D1453435

Women College Basketball Coaches

ALSO BY ROSEMARIE SKAINE
FROM McFARLAND

*Women at War: Gender Issues of
Americans in Combat* (1999)

*Power and Gender: Issues in Sexual
Dominance and Harassment* (1996)

# Women College Basketball Coaches

ROSEMARIE SKAINE

*Foreword by*
BETTY F. JAYNES

McFarland & Company, Inc., Publishers
*Jefferson, North Carolina, and London*

Library of Congress Cataloguing-in-Publication Data

Skaine, Rosemarie.
   Women college basketball coaches / Rosemarie Skaine ; foreword
by Betty F. Jaynes.
     p.    cm.
   Includes bibliographical references and index.
   ISBN 0-7864-0920-7 (softcover binding : 50# alkaline paper) ∞
   1. Basketball for women—Coaching—United States—History.
2. Women basketball coaches—United States—Biography.
3. College sports—United States—History.   I. Title.

GV885.3.S58 2001
796.323'63'082092273—dc21                          2001020238
[B]

British Library Cataloguing data are available

Manufactured in the United States of America

McFarland & Company, Inc., Publishers
  Box 611, Jefferson, North Carolina 28640
  www.mcfarlandpub.com

To my son
F. Todd Skaine,
For his love

# Acknowledgments

I thank the coaches who gave generously of their time to be interviewed for this book. They inspire with their vision, enthusiasm and love for the game.

The coaches' staff members were helpful in facilitating the interviews and providing information that improved the final products. I appreciate their tireless efforts.

I thank the many organizations that provided interviews and material. Special thanks to Maria DeJulio, research staff, NCAA, for her assistance in acquiring various reports.

I thank Robert Kramer, professor emeritus of the University of Northern Iowa, for his assistance in computer technology and programs.

I thank Curtis Nedoba, an avid women's basketball fan, for meaningful direction at the book's inception.

I thank David Hackbart for enabling me to, as Kahlil Gibran said, "watch with serenity through the winters of grief."

I thank my father, Warren V. Keller, for his technological foresight, generosity, and abiding love.

I thank James C. Skaine, my husband, for his editing skills.

I thank Richard L. and Nancy L. Kuehner and William V. and Carolyn E. Guenther Kuehner, cousins, for their tremendous support and love.

I thank Mary Nelson, my friend, who gave support at critical times.

I thank Cass Paley, friend of yesteryear, for the truth that invincibility is within.

# Contents

# *Foreword*

In my very brief but exciting stay in the world of women's sports and specifically women's basketball, I have dreamed of a book like this: a book that would identify people in women's basketball who have given so much of themselves just to give young girls the opportunity to play.

Author Rosemarie Skaine has organized this book in such a way that the reader receives a clear picture of these leaders as sports figures. These figures have contributed to their sport either as researchers, historians, inventors, creators, associate commissioners, commissioners, athletic directors, physical education teachers and professors, or (in the profession that is very dear to my heart) coaches. They instill in the next generation the fire and desire that are needed to continue the escalation of women's sports and the development of girls participating in them.

Sports figures at the top and on the move must be made visible to young girls and boys, allowing them to see that women can be in high leadership roles and still have a life that allows them to be moms, grandmoms, sisters, aunts and wives. I hope and believe that the stories in this book will serve that purpose. Here's to the girls who will be our coaches and leaders in years to come!

*Betty F. Jaynes*

# *Tables*

# Abbreviations

AAU        Amateur Athletic Union
ACC        Atlantic Coast Conference
AIAW       Association for Intercollegiate Athletics for Women
ABL        American Basketball League
BAA        Basketball Association of America
BCA        Black Coaches Association
EADA       Equity in Athletics Disclosure Act of 1994
EEOC       Equal Employment Opportunity Commission
EPA        Equal Pay Act
MVP        Most Valuable Player
NABC       National Association of Basketball Coaches
NACDA      National Association of Collegiate Directors of Athletics
NACWAA     National Association of Collegiate Women Athletic Administrators
NAIA       National Association of Intercollegiate Athletics
NBA        National Basketball Association
NCAA       National Collegiate Athletic Association
OCR        Office for Civil Rights, U.S. Department of Education
WBCA       Women's Basketball Coaches Association

| WBL | Women's Professional Basketball League |
| WNBA | Women's National Basketball Association |
| WISE | Women in Sports and Events |
| WSF | Women's Sports Foundation |

# Preface

*"In the past two decades the growth of women's sports—and
women's basketball in particular—has been unprecedented."*
–Jody Conradt
Head Coach, Women's Basketball
The University of Texas, 1991[1]

Basketball is a highly popular sport, with professional leagues
and stars that are household words.[2] Basketball is popular on every
level and in every variation, says Bob Herzog, whether it be pro, college, high school, women's, the Olympics, the Harlem Globetrotters,
amateur or wheelchair. Frank Dell'apa says that basket ball (two
words) was developed as a diversion, but basketball has become a way
of life. John Wooden, legendary UCLA coach, is not surprised at how
the game has grown, but he admits it is a very different game from
the one he played in the 1920s.

In the women's arena, by 1999 players such as Tennessee All-
American Chamique Holdsclaw and coaches like Pat Summitt of the
Tennessee Lady Volunteers graced the covers of magazines and were
sought out for interviews by the media. Kelli Anderson of *Sports Illustrated* says, "Now that Michael Jordan has left the court, there is no
basketball player, male or female, collegiate or pro, who's in as much
demand as Holdsclaw is right now.... Everyone wants a chunk of
Holdsclaw's time."[3]

7

As a game, Frank Dell'apa reports, basketball "has transcended gender, race and terminology to become one of the world's most popular sports and provides an economic windfall for many involved at the highest levels of the game."[4] Perhaps more than any other segment of the sport, women's basketball reflects the changes that have made the transcendence possible.

Chapter One of this book gives an overview of the early years of women's basketball and how, over time, the game has changed. Chapter Two discusses the changes that came about as a result of Title IX and case law demanding gender equity in sports programs—and how gender equity is still a subject of controversy on many college campuses.

Chapter Three demonstrates how women's basketball has grown from the 1970s to the present. Healthy at the grass roots level (the high school), the game is still growing at the collegiate, professional and international levels. With that growth have come increasingly skilled players who require new coaching strategies. Chapter Three examines these issues, as well as the emergence of professional women's basketball teams.

Chapter 4 is about coaches, administrators and other professionals, both female and male, who have made a difference for women's basketball. Some of the game's best administrators are profiled, and two scholars in the field—the authors of an important longitudinal study of women in intercollegiate sport—discuss their findings regarding changes in the game over a 21-year period.

Chapter 5 profiles selected female coaches of women's college basketball. These coaches and others like them—too many to be profiled here—have shaped the traditions of women's basketball and contributed much to its phenomenal growth.

Chapter 6 offers a look at where the women of the game are taking basketball as we begin the 21st century.

# Introduction

In recent years, women's basketball has experienced phenomenal growth. That growth is measured by the number of women players and women coaches and by their achievements. As more women players elevate their game and as more women coach winning teams, society's interest has grown. The explosive growth is a tribute to the tenacity of the women of the game and their love for women's basketball. It comes also from changes in the game itself, from legislation, from the growth and strength of basketball organizations in combination and from increased coverage by the media. Women played the game indifferent to the fluctuation in rules, but they were not indifferent to the game itself. Title iX of the Education Amendments to the Civil Rights Act of 1964 provided the necessary legislative force to create a social product of more equity for women in sport. Building on that product, the birth of the Women's National Basketball Association (WNBA) and its strategic marketing by the National Basketball Association (NBA) has brought women's basketball into an increasing number of American homes and created more and more fan interest in the college game.[1]

What makes college basketball special is the student athlete. The college coach teaches more than basketball skills; she or he is also preparing the student athlete for life. Coaching occurs on and off the court. Cheryl Miller, former head coach at the University of Southern

California and present head coach and general manager of the Phoenix Mercury (WNBA), says, "Outstanding coaches are those coaches that are not only making an impact on people's basketball skills but also on their personal lives. Living off the court is just as important as on the court."[2]

Christine Grant, athletic director for women's athletics at the University of Iowa, says that there is a philosophical difference between college basketball and pro ball. "In the pro ranks, the aim is to make a profit. That must never, ever be a purpose of intercollegiate athletics. Not ever. What I get concerned about is when we get pushed in that direction, because then, you start making decisions based on money rather than what is best for this student athlete."[3]

Not all of the women's athletic teams are coached by women. In 1990, men coached 53 percent of all women's college sports programs.[4] Yet more than 90 percent of the women's teams had female head coaches in 1972 at the time Title IX was enacted. According to R. Vivian Acosta and Linda Jean Carpenter, "the percentage of women coaching women's teams in 1998 was the second lowest in history" at 47.4 percent. The percentage of women coaching men's teams, they say, "stands at 2 percent and has remained unchanged over the years."[5]

In 1998, women represent 64.6 percent of the women's basketball head coaches in all divisions of NCAA. Acosta and Carpenter say the gender of the head administrator for women's programs "alters the likelihood of finding female coaches coaching women's teams."

Women coaches face economic challenges, and decisions about where and how to coach may be influenced by salary considerations. On the other hand, some female coaches are earning more than they thought possible—even though as a group they may not be earning as much as male coaches—and are facing the competitive odds.

Women coaches of college basketball are, indeed, the women of the game. Their dedication and talent have taken the college game to new heights and will take it even higher.

# Chapter 1

# *History Through the 1960s*

*"The coach has a greater influence in the development of sportsmanship than perhaps any other person with whom the player comes in contact."*
—Alice W. Frymir, Coach
Battle Creek College, Michigan, 1928[1]

The game of basketball was originally designed for male athletes who needed an indoor winter sport. James Naismith created the slow-moving and low-scoring game *basket ball*, which was spelled as two words until 1921. The nine-player teams used a soccer ball for the first game on December 12, 1891, at Springfield, Massachusetts.

Naismith, a physical-education instructor at the YMCA Training School in Springfield, who was assigned the task of creating an indoor game, established that players would move the ball by passing it rather than running (or dribbling) with it. He raised the goals off the floor to prevent collisions, and used peach baskets for goals and ladders to remove the soccer ball. The first public game was played in March 1892. The score? One basket.[2]

That same year, three months after Naismith invented the game, Senda Berenson, Smith College director of physical training, introduced the game to women. The first women's game was played March 22, 1893, at Smith, with a score of sophomores 5, freshmen 4.[3] Naismith's wife, Maude E. Sherman, of Springfield, played in one of the first women's games.[4]

On April 4, 1896, Berkeley University lost to Stanford (3-2) when the teams played the first intercollegiate women's basketball game ever with nine players per team, says Janice Beran.[5] Stanford's Martha Clark made the first basket in women's intercollegiate history. A basket made one point.

The first game quickly changed the rules. The nine-woman team wore very conservative, heavy woolen uniforms that covered all of the body except the face, neck and hands. Roberta Park, chair of the University of California–Berkeley's Department of Physical Education and a specialist in sports history, says, "It wasn't very clear to people in the beginning how the game should be played, so people snatched the ball away from each other, and they didn't know how to throw it into the basket." [6]

On the day of the game, according to basketball historian May Dornin, armory windows were guarded by women holding sticks to keep men from sneaking inside. Only two males were allowed to watch: Walter E. Magee, because he was a physical education instructor who had seen basketball played in Springfield, and Dr. Thomas Wood, director of women's physical education at Stanford.[7] Even letting women watch was apparently considered dangerous: Since basketball was invented for men, physicians who believed women were delicate said women would become hysterical watching other women play basketball.

But those who played found it far from dangerous or intimidating. In 1896, Mabel Craft wrote in the *San Francisco Chronicle*: "The ball is caught and instantly thrown. No one is allowed to fall on it and stay there. Five feet is the farthest you can run with it, and five seconds the longest you can hold it, and all in all, it's the jolliest kind of romp."

## Early Rules

Beran says the first women's rules appeared in 1894, but they were not widely circulated. Evidently the lack of standardization did not concern the players. Those who taught the game, however, were interested in standards and rules. Clara Gregory Baer, a physical educator who in 1893 had introduced basketball at H. Sophie

Newcomb College for Women, New Orleans, published a set of rules called "Basquette" on March 13, 1895.[8] Baer's rules required two teams of six players each, says the WNBA website. Both teams positioned two players in each third of the court. "Legend has it that her rules were based on a misinterpretation of a diagram of the court from hoop daddy James Naismith: she thought that the dotted lines on his diagram used to show where boundaries and shot lines exist were designed to mark off sections of the court."[9]

Senda Berenson, widely acknowledged as the "foremother" of basketball and head of the National Committee on Women's Basketball, worked with other east coast physical education teachers to develop women's rules at the Conference on Physical Training in June 1899 at Springfield, Massachusetts.[10] The rules were published in October 1901. According to the Women's National Basketball Association, Spalding Sporting Goods published Berenson's rules as the "official rules."

## Role Expectations of Players

In a 1992 article by Ron Thomas in the *San Francisco Chronicle*, Roberta Park says that women's roles and their destiny were entirely different from men's. Vigorous, powerful, and strong were masculine role identifiers. Women could not assume these character traits, or if they did, they were violating the rules of nature. Park says that a woman avoided activities that might put her in an ungainly pose or cause her to fall down, since this was not the way a lady should behave. And then there was the threat of sweat: "Women never sweated," says Park. "Horses sweated, men perspired and women glowed."

As an example of how role expectations were expressed in the writings of the day, Park cites Mabel Craft's 1896 *San Francisco Chronicle* article, which dwelled on the fashionable uniforms and emphasized the excellent behavior necessary to demonstrate the game's respectability. In 1910, says Sally Jenkins, women were still wearing long skirts and bloomers exposing no more than fingers, necks and heads. When Berenson invented basketball for women, the words "gender equity" didn't exist, and it would be 30 more years before women could vote. Women often accepted their circumscribed role as readily as men did. They were not to play a man's game like a man. To prevent a woman from losing her graceful, ladylike qualities, Berenson developed rules that not only kept the player in an assigned one-third of the court area, but also "forbade snatching the ball, holding it for more than three seconds, or dribbling it more than three times." [11] Yet, says Jenkins, Berenson favored strenuous activity, partly because one of the most common arguments against women earning equal pay at work was that they were apt to be ill. "They need, therefore," said Berenson, "all the more to develop health and endurance if they desire to become candidates for equal wages."

Uniforms for female players were becoming more practical by the 1920s, noted Alice W. Frymir writing in 1928, and teaching the living of a healthful life remained the responsibility of coaches. Frymir said that the coach, "should instruct the players in the fundamental requirements of diet, sleep, cleanliness, in the cause of underweight and the effect of fatigue, and in a normal attitude toward menstruation and the 'unwisdom' of participating in strenuous activity during at least the first three days of this period. Players should not be made to feel that a 'special' training period is necessary during the basket ball season. Ideally, basket ball, if played, should be a daily activity." [12]

While there wasn't a lot of change in the 1920s, the 1930s brought a "fusion" between athleticism and feminism. Jenkins provides two examples. First, as women in sports gained acceptance, the old passive definitions presented women with a dilemma. Both men and women still thought a woman should care about her appearance. So women simultaneously sought acceptance in athletics while "embracing" cosmetics. Men and women were caught up in the cultural milieu of rising female film stars and Miss America Pageant winners. These cultural tensions fused during a Amateur Athletic Union (AAU) championship tournament competition that named "Beauty Queen of Cage Meet." [13] Secondly, Jenkins says a touring team named "The Red Heads" played exhibitions against men's teams. The women were required "to wear makeup, look beautiful and play well." They were also required to either have red hair, wear red wigs or dye their hair red. In 1999, Tom Weir described the Red Heads from the '30s to the '80s as "the Harlem Globetrotters of the women's game, playing men's rules against men's semipro and military teams." [14] One Red Head basketball player 1962–63, Mickey Childress, says, "We like to think we helped women's basketball stay alive when the colleges were playing our game." [15]

During the '20s, '30s and '40s, the all-black women's barnstorming team the Philadelphia Hustle lost only six times to all-black men's teams while playing men's rules. Ora Washington played for the Hustle for 18 years. Her life gives us another opportunity to gain insight into the fusion of athleticism and feminism. Washington, also a tennis star, had won the all-black American Tennis Association singles titles in 1929, at a time when black athletes were not allowed to profit from sports. Washington worked in domestic service. Upon her retirement she purchased an apartment building and gave free coaching lessons in tennis to neighborhood children.[16]

## The Women's Game

Five-person teams became the standard for men in 1897, and women's teams were reduced from nine to six, say Nelson and Clayton. Women's teams were reduced from six to five players in 1972. Early in basketball's history, the number of players was determined by the size of the court, because the games were played in ill-suited school gyms, churches, or dance halls. In 1938, the three-section court was reduced to two, and in 1971, women could play a full-court game.[17]

Women's basketball underwent significant change from 1962 to 1972. The six-player divided court with three players remaining on each side of the division line progressed to a six-player game with two roving players who could move full length of the court. In 1971, after two years of experimentation, the DGWS–AAU (Division of Girls' and Women's Sports–American Amateur Union) Joint Basketball Rules Committee voted to adopt rules for a five-player game. A rules committee in the National Federation of State High School Associations followed with rules for adoption of the five-player game, which assured all colleges and public schools would play five-player basketball in the future.

## Male and Female Coaches

John Wooden, the legendary former UCLA coach, stacked up a record of 10 NCAA titles, including seven in a row. Herzog credits coaches who are "larger than life" as producing successful programs and college games that reach new heights: Bobby Knight, Dean Smith, John Thompson, and Denny Crum.[18]

Female coaches who developed the game, says Ron Thomas, include Senda Berenson-Abbott (who was inducted into the Naismith Memorial Basketball Hall of Fame in 1985) and Dr. Clelia Duel Mosher, a colleague of Berenson-Abbott in the Smith College women's physical education department who became Smith's director in 1910. Of ten coaches the WNBA lists that we should know, the following contributed to the game either before 1972 or continue to do so in 1999: Clara Baer, Senda Berenson-Abbott, Jody Conradt, Carol Eckman, Theresa Shank Grentz, Billie Moore, Marianne Stanley, and Marian Washington.

These well-known coaches and many like them were in the coaching profession before and after the enactment of Title IX. In spite of Title IX's difficult legal history, they can attest to a steady progress in women's basketball.

# Chapter 2

# *The Era of Title IX*

*"A coach is a coach is a coach."*
—Angie Lee, Head Coach, University of Iowa[1]

Law both reflects and changes society. The antecedent of socio-historical change provides the broader context for understanding law as part of the social order.[2]

The progress of college women's basketball coaches cannot be fully understood without first understanding the larger society's progress in its efforts to view women as the full equals of men. When we apply this concept to the female coach of college women's basketball, we are saying that, as society makes it possible for more women to be coaches, it simultaneously provides the opportunity for others to view these women as competent, qualified coaches of their particular athletic programs.

Title IX also addresses equity for female participants. If we preclude equity at the middle schools and the high schools, realistically, there will be few or no teams at the college level. If there are fewer teams, there is no equity for coaches, thus no opportunity for society to view women as competent athletic participants or qualified professional coaches. Once the opportunity is there, we can recognize an individual on the basis of her competence. The philosophy "A coach is a coach is a coach," stated by University of Iowa coach

Angie Lee, is the same as the philosophy of military women who point out that "a soldier is a soldier," regardless of gender.[3]

## Federal Law

The history of Title IX and the legal activity that followed represents a tremendous struggle and good progress. To view this volatile history in a capsule see Table 2.1.

### TITLE IX

Title IX, the 1972 Educational Amendments to the Civil Rights Act of 1964, states, in part, "No person in the United States shall, on the basis of sex, be excluded from participation in, be denied the benefits of, or be subjected to discrimination under any educational program or activity receiving Federal financial assistance...."[4] The Office for Civil Rights of the United States Department of Education has regulatory responsibility for Title IX. Educational institutions had until 1978 to comply with the law.[5]

In 1996, the Feminist Majority Foundation said that Title IX is the law that "prohibits sex discrimination in federally-funded educational programs, including athletics programs. Schools and colleges receiving federal funds in any part of the institution are required to offer equivalent sports opportunities, equipment, and funding for women's and girls' sports."[6] Mark Conrad of Fordham University's School of Business Administration says that sports was not Title IX's "main thrust." Nevertheless, "the disparity of sports programs for men and women almost cried out for its application."[7]

Title IX, says Conrad, has a difficult legal history. The Department of Health, Education and Welfare (HEW), later reorganized under the Reagan administration into two departments, Health and Human Services and the Department of Education, took three years to enforce Title IX.

Title IX specifies ten factors for the Office for Civil Rights to consider in determining whether institutions are providing equal opportunity in athletic programs. Two of the ten requirements pertain directly to the assignment and compensation of coaches.[8] The factors are

1. selection of sports and levels of competition effectively accommodate the interests and abilities of members of both sexes;

Table 2.1

# History of Title IX Legislation, Regulation and Policy Interpretation

*"No person in the United States shall, on the basis of sex, be excluded from participation in, be denied the benefits of, or be subjected to discrimination under any education program or activity receiving Federal financial assistance."*

| | | |
|---|---|---|
| 1972 | Congress enacted Title IX of The Educational Amendments of 1972 20 U.S.C. ß 1681 et seq. | • Signed into law by President Richard Nixon, June 23, 1972.<br>• Prohibited sex discrimination in any education program or activity receiving any type of Federal financial assistance. |
| 1974 | "Tower Amendment" proposed and rejected. | May 20, 1974, Senator Tower introduced an amendment to exempt revenue-producing sports from being included when determining Title IX compliance. |
| 1974 | "Javits Amendment" enacted & included in the Education Amendments | July 1974, Senator Javits proposed, in lieu of proposed Tower Amendment, a proposal stating HEW (Dept. of Health, Education and Welfare) must issue Title IX regulations which include "reasonable provisions considering the nature of particular sports" e.g., event-management costs, etc. |
| 1975 | O'Hara House Bill H.R. 8394 died in committee | • June 1975, Rep. O'Hara introduced House Bill (H.R. 8394), proposing to use sports revenues first to offset cost of that sport, then to support other sports.<br>• Attempted to alter Title IX coverage in athletics |
| 1975 | HEW issued final Title IX regulation 34 C.F.R. Part 106 | • Signed into law by President Gerald Ford, effective 7/21/75.<br>• Included provisions prohibiting sex discrimination in athletics and established a three year window for educational institutions to comply. |
| 1975 | Congress reviewed and approved Title IX regulations and rejected resolutions disapproving them. | • June 4,1975: the present Title IX regulation was transmitted to Congress.<br>• June 5, 1975, Senator Helms (S. Con. Res. 46), and June 17, 1975, Rep. Martin (H. Con. Res. 310): resolution to disapprove |

| | | entire Title IX legislation<br>• June 17, 1975, Rep. Martin (H. Con. Res. 311), resolution to disapprove Title IX legislation as it related to intercollegiate athletics<br>• July 16, 1975, Senators Laxalt, Curtis & Fannin (S. Con. Res. 52), resolution to disapprove application of Title IX to intercollegiate athletics |
|---|---|---|
| 1975 | Senate refused to act on bills to curtail Title IX enforcement. | July 21, 1975, Senator Helms introduced S. 2146 in an attempt to prohibit the application of Title IX regulations to athletics where participation in those athletic activities are not a required part of the educational institution's curriculum. |
| 1977 | Senate refused to act on bill to curtail Title IX enforcement | January 31, 1977, Senator Helms re-introduced S. 2146 as S. 535. |
| 1977 | A bill attempted to alter Title IX coverage in athletics; it died in committee before reaching House or Senate floors. | July 15, 1977, Senators Tower, Bartlett, & Hruska introduced Senate Bill (S. 2106), proposing to exclude revenue-producing sports from Title IX coverage. |
| 1978 | HEW issued proposed policy "Title IX and Intercollegiate Athletics" for notice and comment; subsequently withdrawn | Presumption of compliance based on substantially equal average per capita expenditures for men and women athletes and future expansion of opportunity and participation for women. |
| 1979 | HEW issues final policy interpretation on "Title IX and Intercollegiate Athletics" 44 Fed. Reg. 71413 et seq. | December 11, 1979: Rather than relying exclusively on the above presumption of compliance standard, the final policy focused on institution's obligation to provide equal opportunity and detailed the factors to be considered in assessing actual compliance. This policy included what is currently referred to as the 3-Prong-Test. |
| 1980 | U. S. Department of Education was established. | DOE was given oversight of Title IX through the Office for Civil Rights (OCR). |
| 1984 | Grove City vs. Bell Decision | This case removed the applicability of Title IX in athletics programs by stating that only those programs or activities which received direct Federal financial assistance be held accountable to Title IX provisions. |

| 1988 | Civil Rights Restoration Act | Became law on 3/22/88 after overriding a Presidential veto by President Ronald Reagan. Overrode Grove City vs. Bell, and mandated that all educational institutions which receive any type of Federal financial assistance, whether it be direct or indirect, be bound by Title IX legislation. |
|------|------|------|
| 1990 | Title IX Investigation Manual | April 2, 1990: OCR, of the U.S. Dept. of Education, published manual. Authored by Valerie M. Bonnette and Lamar Daniel. |
| 1992 | Franklin vs. Gwinnett County Public Schools | February 2, 1992: Supreme Court ruled unanimously that plaintiffs filing Title IX lawsuits are entitled to receive punitive damages when intentional action to avoid Title IX compliance is established. |
| 1992 | NCAA Gender Equity Study | Shortly after Franklin decision, the NCAA completed and published a landmark Gender-Equity study of its member institutions. |
| 1994 | Equity in Athletics Disclosure Act (EADA) Section 360B of Publ.L. 103-382 34 CFR Part 668.41-668-48 Fed. Reg. 11/29/95 p. 61424 | • September 1993: Sponsored by Senator Mosley-Braun (S. 1468) and Rep. Collins (H.R. 921) <br> • Stated that any coeducational institution of higher education that participates in any Federal student financial aid program and has an intercollegiate athletics program must disclose certain information concerning that intercollegiate athletics program. <br> • Annual reports required; first disclosure report was to be available no later than October 1, 1996. |
| 1996 | Policy Clarification | January 16, 1996: OCR issued clarifications of three-part "Effective Accommodation Test" (3-pronged test) |
| 1996 | First EADA Report Due | October 1, 1996: All institutions must have available to all who inquire, specific information on their intercollegiate athletics department as required by the Equity in Athletics Disclosure Act |

Source: "History of Title IX," University of Iowa's Women's Intercollegiate Athletics, June 29, 1999. Online. Internet. Available: http://bailiwick.lib.uiowa.edu/ge/history.html, Nov. 18, 1999.

2. provision of equipment and supplies;
3. scheduling of games and practice time;
4. travel and per diem allowance;
5. opportunities to receive coaching and academic tutoring;
6. assignment and compensation of coaches and tutors;
7. provision of locker rooms, practice and competitive facilities;
8. provision of medical and training facilities and services;
9. provision of housing and dining facilities and services;
10. publicity.

In December 1979, HEW issued policy interpretation to compare equality of opportunity.[9]

Title IX has had a significant effect on sports in American society. Conrad says that overall, Title IX made possible all-women professional basketball leagues including the Women's National Basketball Association (WNBA), increased the popularity of women's sports, and opened sports opportunities for women at all levels in education.

R. Vivian Acosta and Linda Jean Carpenter report that although Title IX brought massive growth in women participating in sports, one effect of the law was not so positive for women: some positions previously held by women, including coaching, became more frequently occupied by men.[10] Acosta and Carpenter's study shows that the percentage of women basketball coaches declined from 79.4 percent in 1977–1978 to 64.6 percent in 1998. (See Table 2.2.)

## The Equal Pay Act

The Federal Equal Pay Act (EPA) is relevant legislation for those individuals affiliated with the administration, teaching and coaching of sports. Coaches may pursue legal action for equal pay through one or more of the following: the Equal Pay Act of 1963, Title VII of the Civil Rights Act of 1964, or Title IX.[11] According to Cathryn Claussen, the Equal Pay Act "prohibits discrimination between employees on the basis of sex by paying different wages for work that is substantially similar in skill, effort, responsibility, and is performed under similar working conditions," whereas Title VII of the Civil Rights Act "prohibits employment discrimination on the basis of race, color, sex, religion, or national origin."[12]

Table 2.2

## Percentage of Female Basketball Coaches, All Divisions

| Year | Percentage | Year | Percentage |
|------|------------|------|------------|
| 1998 | 64.6 | 1987 | 59.9 |
| 1997 | 65.2 | 1986 | 61.0 |
| 1996 | 64.3 | 1985 | 62.7 |
| 1995 | 63.9 | 1984 | 64.9 |
| 1994 | 64.6 | 1983 | 66.6 |
| 1993 | 62.8 | 1982 | 71.2 |
| 1992 | 63.5 | 1981 | 73.7 |
| 1991 | 60.7 | 1980 | 76.5 |
| 1990 | 59.9 | 1979 | 77.7 |
| 1989 | 60.0 | 1977/78 | 79.4 |
| 1988 | 58.5 | | |

*Source: R. Vivian Acosta and Linda Jean Carpenter, "Women in Intercollegiate Sport: A Longitudinal Study—Twenty One Year Update 1977–1998" (Brooklyn, N.Y.: Department of Physical Education and Exercise Science, CUNY, 1998), 1–15.*

In 1995, Lisa A. Bireline Sarver said that because of the growth of women's athletics programs, educational institutions are subjected to much scrutiny for compliance with the EPA to make sure that salaries paid to male and female coaches are equal. She encourages institutions to examine salary inequities that might be based on factors other than gender. In the case of the salary discrepancy of Angela C. Beck, women's basketball coach at the University of Nebraska, the court concluded (despite her spectacular record) that the additional responsibilities of the male teacher in the later years indicated that Beck's position "continued to be different from, and not 'substantially equal' to, the male teacher's job." Because men's basketball was a revenue producing sport, the male coach had significant pressure to have a winning season so that the college would sell more tickets and get more donations.[13]

In 1994, the men's and women's basketball teams at the University of Southern California (USC) faced the salary inequity issue. Marianne Stanley, the head coach of the women's basketball team at USC from 1989 to 1993, said she deserved equal pay with the head men's basketball coach, George Raveling. The courts focused on "differences in responsibility" rather than "skill and effort, as reflected by success," in this case, the success of Marianne Stanley.[14]

After raising the salary issue, Stanley was fired by USC in September 1993.

In 1999, and without trial, the ninth U.S. Circuit Court of Appeals sidestepped the issue in Stanley's case argued in October 1996, and said that "it wasn't necessary to decide whether the job duties of the men's coach were more demanding, because the evidence showed that former USC's men's coach, George Raveling, was more experienced and qualified than Stanley."[15]

In 1995, Phyllis Harker, Utica College's former women's basketball and softball coach, sued, alleging gender discrimination and retaliation. The college said because the male coach had more experience and a greater length of service, his salary was higher. Harker could not disprove this evidence, and the court did not uphold her claim.[16]

The surge of litigation in the mid 1990s, say authors Janet Judge, David O'Brien, and Timothy O'Brien, is due to disgruntled female athletes and female coaches seeking gender parity. Salary disparities based upon a factor other than gender cause the most lawsuits filed under the EPA. The number of lawsuits is not surprising, they say, because "the courts have increasingly shown an intolerance for inequitable opportunities in the high school and collegiate athletic arena." Further, they say that "these suits have helped to define those tangible and intangible aspects of the college coaching position that colleges may lawfully consider when deciding the relative compensation packages for coaches of their male and female programs."[17] Thus, they attempt to provide a practical approach to the coach's compensation package to avoid litigation.

The female coach complainant's first hurdle is to demonstrate that she worked at the same place doing the same work for pay unequal to her male counterpart's. When this is established, say Judge et al., inference of gender discrimination is automatic, and so is the institution's responsibility to defend itself from being liable under many state and federal laws.

The employer then sets out to prove that a female coach was not doing the same work as her male counterpart. The institution will argue that the male basketball coach has to or does generate more funds, has more media coverage, or has more events to attend. Additional pressures warrant a higher salary.

Female coaches in turn argue that fans are attracted to the

male teams' events not because the male coach has "superior abilities," but because the institution has not historically funded or promoted women's basketball. Furthermore, say Judge *et al.*, women are not included in the applicant pool for "high profile men's sports" and are thus not earning the cash.

The courts do not address societal bias, but rather, who has the most responsibility. If the female coach can demonstrate that she is subjected to the same or greater pressures, then there is a new face to the discrimination claim.

Judge *et al.* list vexing pressures that women coaches face that their male colleagues do not, such as societal bias not only against them as coaches, but against the gender of their teams. Should these pressures be considered for compensation?

Judge *et al.* say that the EPA did not mandate comparable worth, a premise "that wages should be based on objective factors rather than market conditions of demand and supply, which may depress wages in jobs primarily held by women as opposed to wages and jobs primarily held by men."[18]

Gregory Szul concludes that ultimately equal pay for coaches "will probably depend less on their actual talents as coaches, but instead, more on the popularity of female athletics. Only then will they command salaries more commensurate with their male counterparts."[19]

## CIVIL RIGHTS ACT OF 1991

The Civil Rights Act of 1991 permits Title VII cases to recover up to $300,000 in compensatory and punitive damages for discrimination and allows a trial by jury.[20]

## PROPOSED FAIR PAY ACT OF 1994

If the Fair Pay Act of 1994[21] had been enacted, Sandra J. Libeson said in 1995, it would have been an evolution of the comparable worth theory and would have provided "women with a statutory framework addressed specifically to comparable worth claims."[22] According to Gregory Szul, the proposed Fair Pay Act of 1994 would have amended the Fair Labor Standards Act of 1938, of which the Equal Pay Act is an amendment. It was an effort to strengthen the Equal Pay Act by extending the protections of that act to race and national origin. More pay can be given on the basis of seniority, but the act defines "equivalent jobs" as "jobs that may be different, but whose requirements are equivalent, when viewed as a composite of skills, effort, responsibility, and working conditions." According to Szul, the Fair Pay Act would have gone beyond the boundaries of the Equal Pay Act: "The Equal Pay Act is restricted to cases of unequal wages for equal work. It does not extend to dissimilar work that is of equal value to an employer akin to a 'comparable worth' standard. The Fair Pay Act of 1994 would remedy this omission through the 'equivalent work' formulation."[23]

### THE EQUITY IN ATHLETICS DISCLOSURE ACT OF 1994 (EADA)

The Equity in Athletics Disclosure Act of 1994 requires schools to make public the participation rates, coaching salaries and expenses, student aid and operating expenses of women's and men's athletic programs. According to the Women's Sports Foundation, these data first became available by individual institution in October of 1996.[24]

### TITLE IX CLARIFICATION STATEMENT BY THE OFFICE FOR CIVIL RIGHTS (OCR), U.S. DEPARTMENT OF EDUCATION

On January 16, 1996, the Office for Civil Rights issued the Title IX Clarification Statement, which keeps and expands upon the three part analysis of equality in athletic opportunities.[25]

### EQUAL EMPLOYMENT OPPORTUNITY COMMISSION (EEOC) 1997 GUIDELINES

In October 1997, the U.S. Equal Employment Opportunity Commission (EEOC) released guidelines that stated that universities must pay the coaches of men's and women's teams similar salaries if their jobs require similar "skill, effort and responsibility."[26] The guidelines have no regulatory power and the EEOC has no enforcement power, but the EEOC can investigate claims and bring court action.[27] Betty Jaynes, CEO of the Women's Basketball Coaches Association, says the EEOC's report determined that salaries should be based not on revenue earned by specific teams, but on experience and responsibility.[28] Ellen J. Vargas, EEOC legal counsel, stated that the commission issued the guidelines to assist both institutions and coaches "Although Congress outlawed sex-discrimination in school programs over twenty-five years ago with the passage of Title IX, recent studies show that the overall pattern of the employment and compensation of coaches by educational institutions is still far from gender-neutral. Because jobs coaching male athletes appear to have been effectively limited to men, the pay disparities between coaches of men's and women's teams raise serious sex discrimination concerns under the employment discrimination laws."[29] Studies show that barely "two percent of the coaches of men's teams are women," and "that men's coaches, overall, substantially out-earn women's coaches in both salaries and benefits." On February 23, 1993, four panelists brought together by the Sports and Entertainment Law section of the Bar Association of San Francisco said that women's sports programs and women coaches had actually lost ground since the 1972 passage of Title IX. The evidence, however, does not fully support that conclusion.[30]

In an interview with the author, Linda Jean Carpenter, professor and attorney, says that the EEOC guidance is "truly very well done. The Guidance pertained to enforcing Title VII and the Equal Pay Act for coaches' salaries. It spelled out some of the excuses that are used for not paying women equally for their work. Because it was so well written, it has given the coaches a sense of 'It's time for me to be treated equally. I've been fighting for my students to be treated equally, now it's time for me. Maybe this is some help for me.'" Carpenter offers arguments against the excuses institutions attempt to use to justify unequal pay. For example, if a school argues that the male teams bring in more revenue, a female coach can respond that she is not given the equivalent support to enable her to raise revenue. If the institution claims that it has consulted with a coach's previous employer to establish a basis for salary, a female coach can point out that her prior salary (like that of her male counterpart) was influenced by sex discrimination.

In a study published in the *Chronicle of Higher Education* (November 14, 1997), Jeffrey Selingo and Jim Naughton say that the EEOC guidelines may have their greatest effect on the salaries of basketball coaches. Certainly there has long been room for improvement in that field. Selingo and Naughton report that "in the 1995–96 academic year, the average base salary of a women's basketball coach was $60,603, 39 per cent less than that of a men's coach." The greatest disparity is at the Division I institutions that have the most competitive athletics programs.

The *Chronicle* reported a salary survey of Division I-A athletics programs conducted by DeLoss Dodds, director of men's athletics at the University of Texas at Austin, that indicates "the median compensation for men's basketball coaches is $290,000, and for women's basketball coaches $98,400." (These figures include not only salaries but income from television, radio, speaking engagements, and the like.) In one example, the male coach of a university's men's basketball team and the female coach of its women's team had similar education, experience, and responsibilities. The university paid the male coach 50 percent more, because the men's team generated considerably more money. The *Chronicle* points out that the men's coach had three assistant coaches and a staff to handle the extra responsibilities, marketing and publicity, while the women's coach had two assistant coaches and no staff.

The Women's Basketball Coaches Association conducted two surveys on women basketball coaches, 1994 and 1997. Their 1997 survey is comparative, comprehensive, and includes all levels of coaching in all divisions.[31] Since there is a thread of consistency in the balance of favor to the coaches of the men's teams, I have selected to address Division I coaches for purposes of this discussion. However, overall, results showed that although coaches of women's teams are getting more annuities in their contracts (1994, 8 percent; 1997, 16 percent), these provisions are more prevalent in contracts of coaches of men's teams (1994, 36 percent; 1997, 35 percent).

Division I experienced a decline in head female coaches (74 percent to 67 percent) and second assistants (87 percent to 81 percent). The salary gap narrowed between 1994 and 1997. Salaries for coaches of the women's teams have increased, but so have salaries of coaches of the men's teams. The average base salary for a women's team coach in 1997 was $69,600, compared to $98,800 for the men's coach. Since 1994, coaches of women's teams have experienced a 24 percent salary increase; coaches of men's teams, 11 percent. Thus, the WBCA concludes the salary gap has narrowed slightly. In 1994 the average salary for coaches of women's teams was $55,828, and for men's teams $88,626, reflecting a $32,798 difference. In 1997, the salary difference was $29,200. The WBCA advises a cautious view of the positive salary gain, pointing out that among those who receive a salary of $100,000 or more, the coaches of men's teams outnumber the coaches of women's teams three to one.

In Division I bonus provisions increased for both coaches, but by dollar amount coaches of the men's team receive a more lucrative bonus. Although women's team coaches have obtained more income through radio and television contracts, there is still a greater difference in the number of men and women receiving contracts, and in the income men's coaches secure from these contracts. In 1997 only 3 percent of women's coaches received $8,000 or more from radio contracts, compared to 20 percent of the men's. Only 12 percent of the women's coaches received television contract income, compared to 39 percent of the men's. While amenities such as country club membership have changed little for coaches of both gender teams, use of an automobile has increased for coaches of women's teams.

In Division I operating budgets for women's teams have increased, but budget allocation is significantly different. In 1997, 45 percent of women's operating budgets fall below $120,000, as compared to 31 percent of men's. Only 15 percent of women's operating budgets exceed $270,000, compared to 34 percent of men's. Although recruiting budgets have increased for women's teams, more dollars are spent for recruiting the male athlete. Travel budgets are shifting a little towards women's teams, but program support still favors the men's team coach.

The Women's Sports Foundation survey on gender equity published in 1997 found that in all divisions men held approximately three-fourths of the full-time and assistant coaching positions. Women constituted 1.9 percent of the head coaches of men's teams, but men held 45 percent of the head coach positions for women's teams. Furthermore, head coaches of women's teams in Division I-A are paid $.63 for every dollar earned by head coaches of men's teams.[32] In addition, the WSF demonstrated that men's sports are not eliminated to increase opportunities for women's sports; female participation opportunities are not in proportion to the number of women in the general student body; female athletes receive less scholarship assistance than their male counterparts; colleges and universities are less committed to recruiting women than to recruiting men to their campuses and athletic programs; and men's teams spend more on operating expenses than women's.

In 1999, the Women's Sports Foundation released another study that addresses issues arising out of the growing popularity of women's sports. The main issue is that the major needs of female athletes, from compensation to adequate training facilities, are not being met. "Many female athletes feel that the low number of female coaches sends the message that women are not taken as seriously as authority figures as men are. While women athletes are functioning as role models for younger girls, they are lacking role models for themselves. There was also some consensus that communication between athletes and coaches would improve if there were more women coaches."[33]

## CASE LAW

Case law acts to interpret existing law. According to Judge *et al.*, in collegiate sports, the most visible pay equity issues have involved female basketball coaches alleging that they have been treated differently by an athletic department on the basis of gender.[34] The body of case law on the subject includes *Haffer vs. Temple University,* brought in 1980 against Temple by the National Woman's law center for non-compliance. This suit represented a challenge to Title IX's progress.[35] According to Diane Heckman, in the 20 year span after Title IX's enactment, "the only decision comparing a women's intercollegiate athletic department to a men's intercollegiate athletic department was rendered in *Haffer*."[36] Most of the remaining handful of decisions, says Heckman, "dealt with the threshold issue of whether the specific program or department received federal funds."

The Temple suit was settled in 1988, but was slowed by another case over Title IX—the issues raised in the *Grove City College* case. In 1984, the U.S. Supreme Court's decision in *Grove City College vs. Bell*[37] addressed whether all school programs are barred from sex discrimination if any activity receives federal funds. The court ruled Title IX had to be interpreted as program-specific. The court's decision had a "chilling effect, particularly on women's athletics," according to Carpenter and Acosta.[38] The Office for Civil Rights (OCR) ceased investigating all Title IX cases. In addition, some colleges and universities withdrew many athletic scholarships for women. The *Grove City* decision left university administrators even more perplexed, because it did not discuss athletics at all, but was about financial aid, say Carpenter and Acosta. In the wake of *Grove City* most claims challenging discrimination in athletics were dismissed.

The Civil Rights Restoration Act of 1987 corrected the "program specific" interpretation problem and said that if any part of a school gets federal funds, Title IX applies to all programs.[39] The Department of Education, as the regulatory agency, reinstated the 1979 rules. According to Conrad, the rules have become the most critical vehicle for interpreting Title IX.[40] John Gibeaut explains that the policy gives three different ways that schools can comply with Title IX:

1. provide opportunities for men and women "in numbers substantially proportionate to their respective enrollments."
2. show a history of program expansion in response to women's developing interests and abilities in sports.
3. show that women's interests and abilities "have been fully and effectively accommodated."[41]

Although compliance rests with the institutions, it is fraught with dilemmas concerning proportionality, participation and budget. An even greater dilemma is posed by the fact that most co-ed campuses have an equal number of women and men students, and that the women's athletics budget is smaller. The players' predicaments are not unrelated to challenges female coaches face.

In 1992, *Franklin v. Gwinnett County Public Schools* made possible claims for compensatory and punitive damages.[42] Christine H. B. Grant, the athletic director for women at the University of Iowa, reminds us that 1992 was also a very important year because the NCAA did a survey to try to determine Title IX's progress in the 20 years since it passed. "People across this nation were shocked at the results."[43] (See Tables 2.3, 2.4, and 2.5.)

One way to assess the impact of Title IX is in revenue production. From 1985 to 1997, basketball's percentage of women's total increased from 13 percent to 21 percent.[44] (See Table 2.6.)

In 1993, *Roberts v. Colorado State University* established that the institution is in compliance if it demonstrates either that opportunities for the gender lesser in number are continually growing, or that the gender breakdown addresses their interests.[45]

In 1996, the court ruled in *Cohen et al. vs. Brown University* that it was not proper to cut teams equally by gender. In 1991, because of budget constraints, Brown University of Providence, Rhode Island, had eliminated two varsity teams of each gender. As a result, female athletes filed a class action discrimination suit. The 1st U.S. Circuit Court of Appeals panel in Boston reaffirmed a

---

Table 2.3

## Changes in Operating Expenses
## (NCAA Gender Equity Survey Results)

| | 1992 | 1997 | Change '91-'92 to '95-'96 | 1999 | Change '95-'96 to '97-'98 |
|---|---|---|---|---|---|
| | | | *Division I-A* | | |
| Men | $1,049,000 | $2,429,000 | $1,380,000 | $1,442,337 | ($986,263) |
| Women | $263,000 | $663,000 | $400,000 | $640,261 | ($22,539) |
| | | | *Division I-AA* | | |
| Men | $415,460 | $589,000 | $173,450 | $490,845 | ($98,155) |
| Women | $139,130 | $270,400 | $131,270 | $280,243 | $9,843 |
| | | | *Division I-AAA* | | |
| Men | $274,740 | $313,800 | $39,060 | $310,734 | ($3,066) |
| Women | $115,850 | $193,900 | $78,050 | $238,719 | $44,819 |
| | | | *Division II* | | |
| Men | $190,470 | $177,500 | $12,970 | $170,957 | ($6,543) |
| Women | $73,300 | $91,500 | $18,200 | $106,412 | $14,912 |
| | | | *Division III* | | |
| Men | $112,400 | $127,200 | $14,800 | $121,368 | ($5,832) |
| Women | $56,120 | $73,400 | $17,280 | $80,200 | $6,800 |

*Source: NCAA, "1997–98 NCAA Gender Equity Study" (Oct. 1999), 32, 44, 56, 68, 80.*

---

Table 2.4

## Proportion of Resources Allocated to Men's and
## Women's Athletic Programs, Division I-A, 1992–1999

| | 1992 | | 1997 | | 1999 | |
|---|---|---|---|---|---|---|
| | M | W | M | W | M | W |
| Participation | 71% | 29% | 66% | 34% | 62% | 38% |
| Athletic Scholarships | 72% | 28% | 66% | 34% | 62% | 38% |
| Operating Budget | 80% | 20% | 79% | 21% | 69% | 31% |
| Recruiting Budget | 84% | 16% | 75% | 25% | 72% | 28% |

*Source: Adapted from NCAA, "1997–98 NCAA Gender Equity Study" (1999).*

Table 2.5

# Proportion of Resources Allocated to Men's and Women's Athletic Programs, Division II and III, 1992–1997

### Division II

| | 1992 | | 1997 | | 1999 | |
|---|---|---|---|---|---|---|
| | M | W | M | W | M | W |
| Participation | 68% | 32% | 65% | 35% | 63% | 37% |
| Operating Expenses | 72% | 28% | 66% | 34% | 62% | 38% |
| Recruiting Expenses | 75% | 25% | 70% | 30% | 67% | 33% |
| Scholarships | 68% | 32% | 64% | 36% | 61% | 39% |
| Head Coaches Salaries | n/a | n/a | 58% | 42% | 55% | 45% |
| Asst. Coaches Salaries | n/a | n/a | 76% | 24% | 74% | 26% |

### Division III

| | 1992 | | 1997 | | 1999 | |
|---|---|---|---|---|---|---|
| | M | W | M | W | M | W |
| Participation | 65% | 35% | 62% | 38% | 60% | 40% |
| Operating Expenses | 67% | 33% | 63% | 37% | 60% | 40% |
| Recruiting Expenses | n/a | n/a | 70% | 30% | 69% | 31% |
| Scholarships | n/a | n/a | n/a | n/a | n/a | n/a |
| Head Coaches Salaries | n/a | n/a | 58% | 42% | 56% | 54% |
| Asst. Coaches Salaries | n/a | n/a | 72% | 28% | 70% | 30% |

*Source: NCAA, "1997–98 Gender Equity Study" (1999).*

Table 2.6

# Trends in Program Revenues, Division 1-A Women's Basketball

### (Dollar Amounts in Thousands)

| Women's Basketball | 1985 | 1989 | 1993 | 1995 | 1997 |
|---|---|---|---|---|---|
| Largest Reported | 136 | 507 | 875 | 1,141 | 1,917 |
| Average | 19 | 58 | 90 | 133 | 174 |
| Percentage of Women's Total | 13% | 8% | 18% | 23% | 21% |

*Source: NCAA, "Revenues and Expenses of Divisions I and II Intercollegiate Athletics Programs: Financial Trends and Relationships—1997" (Overland Park, Kansas: NCAA, Oct. 1998).*

series of district court rulings that Brown was in violation of Title IX, and ordered reinstatement of women's varsity gymnastics and women's volleyball.[46] In 1997, the U.S. Supreme Court let stand the lower court ruling of Brown's violation of Title IX.[47]

Steve Wulf, writing in *Time,* noted the reactions to *Brown* were "swift," "dramatic," and varied.[48] Donna de Varona, Olympic swimmer and first president of the Women's Sports Foundation (WSF), said, "It's the greatest single legal action in the history of women's sports." Mike Garrett, University of Southern California athletic director, felt that it might bring lawsuits against schools earnestly trying to improve women's sports. Donna Lopiano, executive director of the Women's Sports Foundation, said that some people thought salvation would be at hand and Title IX would be overturned. "That was their dream. We hope now that they realize there is no out, that we can move forward and do what we were supposed to do 25 years ago."

Inherent in the *Cohen* decisions and the Title IX controversy is the preservation of football. Deidre G. Duncan says that Title IX's goals can be reached only when male athletes accept some cuts and gender equity proponents do not viciously attack football as the chief sport to cut.[49] Carpenter and Acosta propose that cutting men's participation opportunities is not a creative method of providing gender equity because "athletics participation is a good thing for all who participate."[50]

Lopiano holds that a reduction of the "standard of living" of many football programs would not need to result in lowering participation opportunities or scholarship support. There is no need, she says, to choose between our sons and daughters. Gender equity does not equate with football's demise.[51]

Brown University chose to fight a case on one narrow issue, which was the issue of proportionality, says Linda Carpenter. "Brown couldn't meet the other two [requirements], and they seemed to forget that the third, the proportionality one, was given to institutions as a safe harbor. They fought, but ultimately, the Supreme Court rejected the case."[52]

*Cohen et al. v. Brown University* was one of two major Title IX cases women won. California State University settled the class action lawsuit that was filed in February 1993 in a California state court, *California Chapter of National Organization for Women v. Board of Trustees for the California State University System,* by consenting to comply with Title IX by 1998–99. Diane Heckman describes the case against the entire California State University system as "the most ambitious litigation involving gender equity in intercollegiate athletics."[53] She explains that "the complaint alleged violation of California state statutes, which require gender equity, and a violation of the equal protection clause of the California State Constitution." At the same time, a companion lawsuit began in another California state court challenging gender equity in the athletic department at San Jose State University in *California National Organization for Women v. Evans*.[54] The consent decree settlement is notable because it governed all of the California State University system of twenty post-secondary schools. The settlement was more lenient than Title IX and allowed the state schools five years (by 1998–99) to come into compliance.

## TRENDS

Through case law in all sports, we see that people used Title IX to change intercollegiate athletics and put women's sports on more of an equal basis with men's. These people took their universities to court and made a difference. For example, *Cohen v. Brown* was not focused directly on basketball, but it is the most important litigation to date on gender discrimination in intercollegiate athletics, says Jim Naughton.[55]

Cathryn Claussen notes a shift in Title IX litigations from "participation opportunities for female athletes" to "other issues, such as reverse discrimination, retaliatory firings of coaches, and salary disparities between male and female coaches."[56] Sanya J. Tyler, the women's basketball coach at Howard University in Washington, D.C., was the first to win a jury award through Title IX.[57] Ultimately, she received a reduced award of $1.1 million in her damage suit against Howard University.[58] Claussen explains that Tyler received the award under the Equal Pay Act and sued, along with other complaints, for sex discrimination for paying her a salary lower than that of the men's basketball coach. In *Pitts v. Oklahoma*, the court found violations of sex discrimination under Titles VII and IX because the women's golf coach at Oklahoma State University earned $35,712, while the men's golf coach earned $63,000.[59]

If part of the reason a program is not compliant is that the program doesn't have enough coaches of women's teams, the institution may be required to hire several coaches at the same time. "The added coaches will not necessarily be women," says Claussen, whose research "suggests that female coaches are as qualified as male coaches." She maintains that intercollegiate salaries are lower for coaches of women's teams regardless of the coach's gender. NCAA Gender Equity study figures support her conclusion. (See Table 2.7.) Thus salary disparity issues must be treated under Title IX, rather than just under Title VII and the Equal Pay Act, "because many males coach women's teams, it would be difficult under both laws to prove that a women's coach was discriminated against simply on the basis of being female, rather than because the team she coached was female." On the other hand, the coaching position of females must be examined. (See Table 2.8 and Table 2.9.)

In 1997, *New York Law School Journal of Human Rights* reported that "the average base salary for a coach of a women's athletic team ($44,961) is just fifty-nine percent of the average base salary for a coach of a men's athletic team ($76,566)."[60] In 1999, Lopiano found that in basketball the percentage of women coaches declined from 1978 to 1997. In 1978 the percent of women coaches

---

Table 2.7

## Coaches' Salaries in Men's and Women's Basketball, 1997 and 1999

|  |  | Head Coaches | | | Assistant Coaches | | |
| Division | Yr | Men's Teams | Women's Teams | N/ team | Men's Teams | N/ team | Women's Teams |
|---|---|---|---|---|---|---|---|
| I-Overall | 97 | $99,283 | $60,603 | 2.7 | $95,040 | 2.4 | $62,530 |
|  | 99 | $120,857 | $74,187 | 2.9 | $113,345 | 2.7 | $80,031 |
| I-A | 97 | $128,836 | $78,340 | 2.9 | $127,385 | 2.7 | $84,502 |
|  | 99 | $164,927 | $100,235 | 3.0 | $152,762 | 3.0 | $106,989 |
| I-AA | 97 | $76,979 | $49,003 | 2.5 | $72,996 | 2.2 | $50,102 |
|  | 99 | $88,439 | $56,377 | 2.8 | $82,955 | 2.6 | $60,811 |
| I-AAA | 97 | $92,098 | $53,455 | 2.7 | $83,393 | 2.3 | $50,717 |
|  | 99 | $100,911 | $60,098 | 2.9 | $97,707 | 2.5 | $66,663 |
| II | 97 | $38,287 | $30,644 | 1.6 | $18,352 | 1.4 | $14,430 |
|  | 99 | $38,576 | $31,590 | 1.6 | $19,500 | 1.5 | $16,669 |
| III | 97 | $22,853 | $19,446 | 1.8 | $6,912 | 1.5 | $5,269 |
|  | 99 | $22,319 | $18,745 | 1.7 | $7,049 | 1.5 | $5,535 |

*Source: NCAA, "Gender-Equity Study: Summary of Results (April 1997); NCAA "1997–98 Gender-Equity Study" (Oct. 1999).*

Table 2.8

## Numbers of Full-time and Part-time Basketball Coaches, 1997

| | Men's Teams | | | | | | | | Women's Teams | | | | | | | |
|---|---|---|---|---|---|---|---|---|---|---|---|---|---|---|---|---|
| | *Male* | | | | *Female* | | | | *Male* | | | | *Female* | | | |
| Div | n | FT | n | PT | n | FT | n | PT | n | FT | n | PT | n | FT | n | PT |
| *Head Coaches* | | | | | | | | | | | | | | | | |
| I-A | 92 | 1.0 | 0 | | 0 | | 0 | | 28 | 1.0 | 0 | | 62 | 1.0 | 0 | |
| I-AA | 98 | 1.0 | 4 | 1.0 | 0 | | 0 | | 37 | 1.0 | 5 | 1.0 | 56 | 1.0 | 3 | 1.0 |
| I-AAA | 69 | 1.0 | 0 | | 0 | | 0 | | 28 | 1.0 | 0 | | 38 | 1.0 | 1 | 1.0 |
| II | 166 | 1.0 | 42 | 1.0 | 0 | | 0 | | 67 | 1.0 | 30 | 1.0 | 89 | 1.0 | 21 | 1.0 |
| III | 153 | 1.0 | 110 | 1.0 | 0 | | 0 | | 38 | 1.0 | 48 | 1.0 | 112 | 1.0 | 69 | 1.0 |
| *Assistant Coaches* | | | | | | | | | | | | | | | | |
| I-A | 91 | 2.6 | 32 | 1.1 | 0 | | 0 | | 46 | 1.0 | 9 | 1.1 | 87 | 2.0 | 24 | 1.0 |
| I-AA | 96 | 2.0 | 65 | 1.2 | 0 | | 0 | | 31 | 1.2 | 21 | 1.1 | 76 | 1.6 | 47 | 1.2 |
| I-AAA | 68 | 2.3 | 36 | 1.1 | 0 | | 0 | | 27 | 1.4 | 10 | 1.1 | 52 | 1.6 | 30 | 1.0 |
| II | 95 | 1.0 | 155 | 1.7 | 0 | | 2 | 1.0 | 19 | 1.0 | 70 | 1.2 | 53 | 1.0 | 118 | 1.2 |
| III | 42 | 1.1 | 243 | 1.9 | 0 | | 2 | 1.0 | 8 | 1.0 | 99 | 1.2 | 27 | 1.0 | 188 | 1.4 |

Legend:
    n = number of institutions reporting
    FT = full-time coach
    PT = part-time coach

*Source: NCAA "Gender-Equity Study: Summary of Results" (Apr. 1997).*

was 79.4 percent, compared to 1997 when it was at 65.2 percent.[61] Thus, says Lopiano, we not only find a salary discrepancy, but also a decrease in female coaches.

In some cases, people have not won in pursuing equity. In 1983, Charlene Sennewald, a part-time assistant coach of the women's softball team at the University of Minnesota, was denied in her effort to be full-time. The University did grant full-time appointments to the male assistant coach of women's gymnastics and to two female assistant coaches of the women's basketball and volleyball teams. The 8th Circuit court refused to overturn the ruling against Sennewald, who complained she was discriminated against because of her sex.[62]

The 1990s presented a picture of ongoing Title IX litigation relevant to women coaches, and an equal number of legal scholarly articles. Grace-Marie Mowery says that although most of Title

**Table 2.9**

## Numbers of Full-time
## and Part-time Basketball Coaches, 1999

| | Men's Teams | | | | | | | | Women's Teams | | | | | | | |
| | Male | | | | Female | | | | Male | | | | Female | | | |
| Div | n | FT | n | PT | n | FT | n | PT | n | FT | n | PT | n | FT | n | PT |
| --- | --- | --- | --- | --- | --- | --- | --- | --- | --- | --- | --- | --- | --- | --- | --- | --- |
| *Head Coaches* | | | | | | | | | | | | | | | | |
| I-A | 90 | 1.0 | 0 | 0 | 0 | | | | 23 | 1.0 | 1 | 1.0 | 66 | 1.0 | 1 | 1.0 |
| I-AA | 84 | 1.0 | 7 | 1.0 | 0 | | 0 | | 29 | 1.0 | 5 | 1.0 | 53 | 1.0 | 1 | 1.0 |
| I-AAA | 56 | 1.0 | 2 | 1.0 | 0 | | 0 | | 20 | 1.0 | 1 | 1.0 | 35 | 1.0 | 0 | |
| II | 139 | 1.0 | 93 | 1.0 | 0 | | 0 | | 50 | 1.0 | 46 | 1.0 | 78 | 1.0 | 53 | 1.0 |
| III | 57 | 1.0 | 218 | 1.0 | 0 | | 0 | | 13 | 1.0 | 68 | 1.0 | 40 | 1.0 | 147 | 1.0 |
| *Assistant Coaches* | | | | | | | | | | | | | | | | |
| I-A | 91 | 2.9 | 18 | 1.1 | 0 | | 0 | | 52 | 1.0 | 5 | 1.0 | 88 | 2.1 | 19 | 1.1 |
| I-AA | 83 | 2.2 | 53 | 1.4 | 0 | | 0 | | 34 | 1.2 | 13 | 1.2 | 73 | 1.7 | 44 | 1.2 |
| I-AAA | 57 | 2.4 | 28 | 1.1 | 0 | | 0 | | 17 | 1.1 | 6 | 1.0 | 51 | 1.9 | 22 | 1.1 |
| II | 88 | 1.2 | 201 | 1.8 | 0 | | 2 | 1.0 | 17 | 1.0 | 102 | 1.2 | 55 | 1.2 | 135 | 1.3 |
| III | 16 | 1.4 | 255 | 2.0 | 0 | | 5 | 1.0 | 1 | 1.0 | 116 | 1.2 | 13 | 1.2 | 208 | 1.4 |

Legend:
            n = number of institutions reporting
            FT = full-time coach
            PT = part-time coach

*Source: NCAA, "1997-98 NCAA Gender-Equity Study" (Oct. 1999).*

IX's focus is on the female athlete, the law's intent is to have a similar benefit on female coaches.[63] She adds that a "glass sneaker" is developing in the hiring of female coaches and that, although little case law addresses this issue, the disparity between the number of male and female coaches is well documented. She cites studies and an early 1997 ESPN broadcast that reported a 185 percent increase in the number of jobs coaching female athletes after the passage of Title IX, and adds that 98 percent of these jobs were filled by men. Mowery explores the causes of discrimination, but she focuses on how Title IX may be a legal remedy for the disparity in the numbers of female and male coaches through supporting the establishment of an affirmative action hiring plan in an athletic program. She says that with increasing female athletic participation, the need for female coaches is a corollary. Thus, a hiring plan should be in effect that would not endanger male counterparts.

In 1998, a women's basketball coach sued the City University of New York because her salary was less than that of a male basketball coach. The plaintiff alleged that she was removed as Women's Athletics Coordinator in retaliation. The court held that the coach was equal in skill, effort and responsibility to the male coach. She was entitled to back pay for the differences in salary, as well as liquidated and compensatory damages.[64] In a similar case at Texas A&M, the court held "in part" for the coach for pay and retaliation.[65]

Sometimes people make a difference without going to court or without the threat of litigation. For example, Sherry Winn, a coach at the University of Southern Colorado in Pueblo, was fired over allegations about her sexuality, but the university president reinstated her.[66] The position of Georgia Tech's first women's basketball coach, Bernadette McGlade, came about because athletics director Homer Rice made complying with the educational amendments a priority when he arrived in 1980.[67] In the 1994-95 season, $42,000 a year coach Jody Runge, University of Oregon, threatened legal action to gain equity with the men's game in terms of salary and team status.[68] By 1999, Runge's base salary was $140,000, with a total compensation package possibly exceeding $200,000.[69] Many schools work assiduously to remain in compliance and therefore do not draw the media's attention.

## Special Considerations

### AFRICAN AMERICAN WOMEN COACHES

In salary equity, however, white female coaches as a group have not reached parity. A brief look at African American female coaches demonstrates that neither have they reached parity with male counterparts.

In a 1998 article in the *Howard Law Journal*, Tonya M. Evans argues that Title IX "provides a remedy to black women, but only to the extent they are injured by the force of gender discrimination like that faced by white women."[70] Black women, she says, have a unique history, and they have not been afforded early participation in sports due to their low socio-economic status and the overt discrimination against them. Unless Title IX addresses the black woman, it does not adequately address gender. Evans's research found that college African American women are but a small proportion of those participating in sports, and are usually typecast into only a handful of sports. Racism is a reflection of the larger society.

Sports are important to all. Evans found that "in 1971, 30,000 women were participating in sports. The number increased to 135,000 women as of 1997. Additionally, participation of high school aged girls grew from 300,000 in 1971 to approximately 2.4 million in 1997."[71]

If African American women have traditionally been under-represented in athletics, then their opportunities to be coaches will also be limited. In 1994, according to *Ebony*, women's basketball did not receive the public recognition the game deserves, and collegiate coaches did not bring in the salaries their talents have earned. But the news is not all bad, for in spite of these obstacles, "black women are among the leading basketball coaches at predominantly white and historically black institutions."

*Ebony* reports that leading coach Vivian Stringer admits the obstacles are there, but they didn't stop her from getting the same salary as the male coach at Iowa University, or from making a spectacular record as a coach who in 1994 had "capped 11 head coaching years at the University of Iowa ... with her 500th career victory."[72]

In addition to Stringer, the top 10 leaders in the NCAA Division in 1994 included Marian Washington, a 21-year head coach at the University of Kansas and the first black to coach women at a predominantly white school; Cheryl Miller, University of Southern California; Jessie Kenlaw, University of Houston, Charlene Curtis, Temple University; and Marianna Freeman, Syracuse University. In black schools, Shirley Walker, head coach, Alcorn State University, has 200-plus wins, and Patricia Bibbs, Grambling State University, has over 160 career wins.

## GENDER DIFFERENCES

In 1998, C. Bonnie Everhart and Packianathan Chelladuria published a survey of 97 female and 94 male basketball players that showed gender differences did not affect coaching self-efficacy, occupational valence and perceived barriers.[73] Their research also showed that, despite the increase in female participants and coaching positions, there has been a pervasive decline in the proportion of women in the coaching ranks at all levels of educational institutions. Although their study focused on the reduced entry rate of female coaches, the coaches' faster exit rate is also a reason for the reduced proportion. The authors chose basketball for their study because they found it to be the most popular women's sport among collegiate athletic programs. Their study did not reveal gender differences in coaching as a cause for the underrepresentation of women in the coaching ranks.

Nor did they find that the cause resides in the women participating in sports. Female participants coached by women experience less discrimination and have more desire to become coaches. The Everhart and Chelladuria study certainly bears out the importance of the interrelationship of the female participant and the female coach.

Everhart and Chelladuria list several reasons other researchers have given for the decline in the proportion of female coaches: "women's perceptions of the success of the old boys' club network, lack of support systems for females, failure of the old girls' club network, and women leaving coaching and administrative positions sooner than men; administrators' perceptions of the lack of qualified female coaches, a failure of women to apply for job openings, the lack of qualified female administrators, and time constraints due to family obligations[74]; experienced burnout[75]; preferences of male and female athletes for a male coach[76]; the increased attraction coaching women's teams has for male coaches[77]; homologous reproduction by men[78]; long hours of work; lack of success experienced by women[79]; and both current and former coaches perceived higher levels of satisfaction from alternative activities than from coaching itself."[80]

Women coaches, like other women in our society, stay or leave coaching for the same reasons that men do, because men and women usually work for the same reasons: economic security, career fulfillment and personal satisfaction. But women's basketball, like every career, raises its own unique issues. Among the women that I interviewed there is a dedication to preserving the women's game. The women's game is one of skill and finesse. Although some believe that it does not matter what the gender of a coach is, others argue that it does make a difference. Although female coaches' base salaries are becoming more equitable with male coaches, their total salary package is not. Men coaches easily infiltrate the positions of coaching women's basketball, but women are not so mobile. So within the women coaches of the women's game there are critical issues. While some women want to keep their game, others want to emulate men.

To Christine H. B. Grant at the University of Iowa, equal does not mean identical. "Equality to me means my right as a woman to define my destiny." Grant says that she does not agree with women who want to emulate the model of the men's game:

> I don't agree with football and men's basketball being treated like gods, and others being treated as second class citizens. That's what I dislike about women's basketball right now: that there are some in the game who, as long as they've got what they want—the huge salaries, the huge financial compensation, the television shows, the radio shows, the Nike contracts—find that's where their goals lie. That has never been my goal, and never, ever will be. I disagree with the basketball coach being paid twice as much as the next coach who may be way better than she is or he is. We have to make a concerted effort not to go in this direction. Coaches in women's basketball teams should, in my opinion, should not be clamoring for identical practices to the men's if they are really concerned for student athletes.[81]

Grant believes colleges are being forced to classify sports as "major" and "minor" and treat them accordingly.

> It's not just the difference in salaries [but] that is one huge thing.... Why should somebody at a college level who happens to coach a sport that the public likes make three or four or five times more than a coach who is equally successful in all areas, but in a sport that the public just doesn't happen to like? That's totally irrelevant. It would be very relevant in pro sport. It is not relevant on the college campus. I see that as the biggest obstacle in creating our informed model of sport for everybody.

There's no doubt about it, college coaches are under increasing pressure. The media's increased involvement increases the level of scrutiny of women's basketball, thus contributing to raised expectations, pressures, and responsibility. All these changes have to be managed. But if you want the growth of the game, you welcome the changes, says Bernadette V. McGlade, the assistant commissioner of women's basketball operations for the Atlantic Coast Conference. "The expectations of women's basketball coaches, the expectations they have of themselves as well as the expectations that others such as administrators have of them, also contribute to the pressure. It is a great responsibility that comes with the growth the game."[82]

In addition to the change in media coverage, the coaches' responsibilities in recruiting have probably changed the most, says Ceal Barry, the head coach of women's basketball at the University of Colorado in Boulder:

> Twenty years ago, Division I had what was called an open audition which was allowable under AIAW rules. Letters were sent to 150 of the top high school players within driving distance of the university. They would come to your university to audition or try out. At the end of the day, you would pick 10 of them or so and walk them around your campus to try to influence them to come to your school. There was minimal letter writing, phone calling, or visiting. As a matter of fact, you weren't even allowed to go off your campus to recruit a player. Now, you have two full-time staff members who have 95 percent of their job responsibility in recruiting, and it may take one coach in almost a full-time capacity to recruit one player. It's a total change. It's image, a lot more image; marketing, sales, the use of your web site, email, that one-on-one attention.[83]

Rene Portland, the head coach of women's basketball at Penn State, says that the responsibility of coaches is greater. Coaching went from part time to full time. Although she has more staff, she says, "we are asked to do a lot of fund raising, not necessarily for your budget, but for the university; and a lot of speaking engagements and a lot of recruiting." In addition Portland says that the student athletes of 20 years ago were good for their time, but the quality of athletes in 1999 is unbelievable in comparison.[84]

Regardless of why a coach may stay or go, she is faced with many pressures that create her image. Barbara Stevens of Bentley College in Waltham, Massachusetts, believes communication skills are critical to good coaching. "Relating to your players is as important as the information that you give to them, and how you give it is probably more important."[85] She says that the biggest changes occur in terms of the athletes, because every year "you have a

Ceal Barry, head coach of women's basketball at the University of Colorado.

Rene Portland, head coach of Penn State's Lady Lions, in conference with player Maren Walseth. (Photograph: Steve Manuel.)

different group of kids, your chemistry changes, your personnel changes and the players themselves have different issues than maybe they did back 20 years ago. Society has changed. Coaches have to recognize that what was a common coaching strategy that would have worked then maybe doesn't work now. Maybe there's just different people with different issues from different backgrounds. You have to understand and make an adjustment as a coach, depending on who it is you are coaching."

So does it matter whether a male or a female coaches a women's basketball team? Beliefs are mixed. Some coaches interviewed believe there is a better understanding when the coach is the same gender as the players, and that having a same gender role model is important. Some are very pragmatic in that they equate preserving the women's game for women coaches and women players with their own economic survival. Grant says:

> When I became athletic director [at Iowa] in 1973, I was fairly naive, and I thought that with the explosion of the women's sports we would see men being hired for women's sports but we'd also see women being hired for men's sports. Richard Lapchick's racial and gender analysis reported that men have retained 98 percent of all coaching positions in men's athletics and now have taken over 52 percent of all coaching positions in women's athletics. So, they kept almost 100 percent of one pie, and now they've got more than half of the other. Is that important? I think that it's vitally important.[86]

Grant believes that women come up with entirely different ways of thinking about sports that are extremely beneficial to the sport for boys and girls, men and women. Furthermore, she believes, if we do not hire women, we lose half the brain power of this nation.

Others believe that the gender of the coach is irrelevant to good coaching for either men and women. However, WSF director Donna Lopiano expounds on the ability question and adds strength to Grant's position that men are gaining more coaching positions than women:

> No, I don't think it makes a difference whether a team has a female or male coach. I think discrimination, however, is occurring. You would expect in a non–gender discriminatory situation that you would find equal numbers of male and female coaches coaching both men's and women's teams. This is true in the coaching of women's teams, but is far from true in the coaching of men's teams, so discrimination is occurring in places where you might not think of looking. It's in the coaching of men's teams, not the coaching of women's teams.[87]

So why do athletic administrators hire male coaches? Kerri-Ann McTiernan, coach of the men's basketball team at Kingsborough Community College, says that top male coaches get called with job offers even though everyone knows that they are not leaving their positions:

"Would you consider coming here, would you consider coming there?" Yet, when athletic directors are asked, "Did you call such-and-such female head coach? Did you call women in the game? Well, why not?" "Well, I never thought of it." That's generally the answer given. To me, that's mind boggling. It's unproven right now, but I'm just shocked that someone hasn't found the best candidate [to take a top job] to be a woman. It's a huge risk to take, I guess, as an athletic director because you know there's going to be national, probably international attention. You're sitting there as the one who hired the person, but I cannot see how that could be a failure.

In 1990, Bernadette Locke-Mattox became the first woman to coach a men's basketball program at the NCAA's highest level when she became an assistant to Rick Pitino at the University of

In the huddle with her team is Kerri-Ann McTiernan, head coach of men's basketball for Kingsborough Community College of the City University of New York.

Kentucky. In 1992 Leslie Crandell, former player at Stanford University, became an assistant coach at Westmont College, a member of the small-college National Association of Intercollegiate Athletics.[88] Nancy Lieberman-Cline became the first woman to play in a men's professional league in 1986. She played for the U.S. Basketball League's Springfield Fame for one year, and then for the Washington Generals.[89]

### SCHOLARSHIPS AND FINANCING

One of the obstacles for the female participant is getting a fair share of the scholarships. In 1987, The *Chronicle of Higher Education* reported that the NCAA ruled that its members cut the number of players on scholarships from 15 to 13 in men's and women's basketball.[90] On a brighter note, in 1998, *New York Law School Journal of Human Rights* noted that in keeping with the rising number of intercollegiate women athletes, the number of athletic scholarships available for women increased from 60 in 1974 to approximately 500 in 1981.[91]

# New Frontiers

### CORPORATE COFFERS

Donna Lopiano says that the next frontier is the nation's corporate coffers, reports Wayne Coffey.[92] Without significant investors, Lopiano believes, women's sports will be marginalized no matter how good they are. Judy Foudy, co-captain of the U.S. women's soccer team, says that the U.S. Soccer Federation finally took a risk and aggressively marketed the team by placing its opening event in the larger Giants Stadium as opposed to a smaller 5,000-seat stadium. Ultimately, the championship playoff took place in the Rose Bowl stadium that seated approximately 90,000. Even President Clinton attended. Thus, the World Cup promotional and media buildup made a difference.

Although college basketball players and coaches cannot accept corporate funds, they are dependent upon adequate funding. Dissenting Judge Harry Pregerson in *Stanley vs. University of Southern California* called the university's promotion of the women's basketball program "half-hearted" and its marketing of the men's basketball program "intensive."[93] One has to pose the question whether adequate funding for women's college basketball programs is part of the package for successful coaches and their programs.

Total contract equity promises to be elusive. Some top women's coaches may be making the same base salary as their counterparts in the men's game, but sports writer Vicki Michaelis says that contract equity is "far from a bygone issue." Betty Jaynes, WBCA, says, "Things are beginning to move forward, but we're not there yet and I don't know if we ever will be 100 percent tit for tat."[94] Jaynes estimates that base salaries are equal in less than 10 percent of Division I institutions, and even then, a wide gap in additional benefits exists. According to Michaelis, the U.S. General Accounting Office found that women's basketball coaches earned only 25 percent of the average additional benefits paid to men's coaches.

According to Dick Tharp, University of Colorado athletic director, the factors that drive the market value beyond base salary are "usually generated by money."[95] The university spends the same amount of money on each team, and ticket sales generate about the same amount for each team, but the men's team gets enough money to break even for the season from payouts from conference and NCAA tournaments. The payouts for the Big 12 women's teams are minuscule by comparison because women's basketball doesn't have the multimillion-dollar television contracts that men's teams have. Total contract equity is an exception.

## Mixed Gender Teams

Mixed gender teams may not be so new at lower levels of education,[96] but making their way through athletics at a higher level is a little more difficult. While many women players have the necessary skill levels, the men's game is a physical game; supposedly not a contact sport, it has become just that. As a group, physically the men are stronger, taller, faster, and quicker. The emphasis must be placed on the words "as a group," because there are women who have played, and played well, on men's teams. And of course, many men do not qualify to play on men's basketball teams.

When asked about mixed gender teams, many advocates of women's basketball also stress the importance of preserving the women's game, with its unique qualities. Players and coaches say that the women's game is one of finesse, played below the rim, while the men's game is one of slamming and dunking and played above the rim. Lynn Bria at the Ohio University at Athens says it best:

> I don't think that women will ever be playing on what are considered the men's teams. But why would we want to? I've always been a big believer—and I still am—that in women's basketball we need to establish our own game. What is wrong with that? I never understood why we have always felt the need to be like the men. I think we can learn from what the men do. We can take some things they do, what we like, that will promote our game and help people and make our game interesting. Right now our game is so pure. It's a great game to watch. I've never understood why we've always, always got to make changes or be like the men and make changes because they make changes. We need to kind of run our own race, so to speak. The players and the people that are watching our game should have a voice in changes, but I don't think that we should make changes just because the men do, or that we need them, or that we need to play on the same team.[97]

## Conclusions

The years since Title IX have not been without struggle, but they have been years of progress. The Office for Civil Rights (OCR) says that there is a fourfold increase in women's athletic participation since 1971; that in 1995 women comprised 37 percent of college student athletes, compared to 15 percent in 1972; that in 1996, 39 percent of all high school athletes were female, compared to 7.5 percent in 1971 (representing an eightfold increase); and that women won a record 19 Olympic medals in the summer of 1996.[98] In the 2000 Olympics, American women broke that record by winning 39 medals, according to the ESPN "Medal Tracker."

Although there have been three major pieces of supporting and related legislation—The Women's Educational Equity Act of 1974, Title VII of the Civil Rights Act of 1964, and the 1976 amendments to the Vocational Education Act of 1963—and much additional legal activity as outlined in this chapter, pay in coaching still needs to be made more equitable, and women need to be provided equal access to positions traditionally reserved for men, such as coaching men's teams that are generally considered revenue producing. Only as women coaches are afforded the opportunity to not only do the same work as men, but be paid the same as men, will society begin to recognize women coaches as competent professionals. Importantly, society will then be fully utilizing more of its women members' talents, thus growing stronger as a nation.

# Chapter 3

# *History 1970–1999*

*"Sport is a global cultural institution."*
Donna A. Lopiano, Executive Director[1]
Women's Sports Foundation

## The Game

In 1972, the first Association for Intercollegiate Athletics for Women (AIAW) national tournament was held. In 1976, women's basketball became, for the first time, an Olympic medal sport at the summer games in Montreal.[2] The collegiate women's game grew with the introduction of an NCAA Tournament in 1982. On December 21, 1984, Georgeann Wells, West Virginia, became the first woman to dunk in a college game. One year later, on November 13, 1985, Lynette Woodard became the first woman to play for the Harlem Globetrotters. Old Dominion University's Nancy Lieberman from Far Rockaway, New York, became the first female member of a men's professional team in 1986, the United States Basketball League's Springfield Fame.

The increasing accomplishments of women in sports inspired various organizations to give them recognition. In 1983, Converse athletic outfitters first presented the prestigious Coach of the Year Award for the Women's Basketball Coaches Association (WBCA).

Since then three coaches have been multiple winners: Pat Summitt (3), Jody Conradt and Vivian Stringer (2 each). The WBCA Coach of the Year Award is presented annually to one coach in each of the collegiate divisions—Division I, Division II, Division III, NAIA and JC/CC—as well as high school winning coaches are those who best fulfill the following criteria: "team success during current season, team improvement from previous season, fulfillment of team potential, and professional manner and attitude of coach."[3] The selections are made from the winners of the District Coach of the Year Award in Divisions I, II, III and NAIA, JC/CC and high school. (See Table 3.1.)

In 1984 the National Organization for Women (NOW) believed that the Naismith Basketball Hall of Fame should include women among its 143 electees. Women had been nominated but had never won the needed 12 votes of the committee. Senda Berenson Abbott was nominated and rejected six times.[4] In 1985, Berenson Abbott

---

Table 3.1

## WBCA Coach of the Year 1983–2000

| Year | Coach | School |
|------|-------|--------|
| 1983 | Pat Summitt | Tennessee |
| 1984 | Jody Conradt | Texas |
| 1985 | Jim Foster | St. Joseph's, Pennsylvania |
| 1986 | Jody Conradt | Texas |
| 1987 | Theresa Grentz | Rutgers |
| 1988 | Vivian Stringer | Iowa |
| 1989 | Tara VanDerveer | Stanford |
| 1990 | Kay Yow | North Carolina State |
| 1991 | Rene Portland | Penn State |
| 1992 | Ferne Labati | Miami-Florida |
| 1993 | Vivian Stringer | Iowa |
| 1994 | Marsha Sharp | Texas Tech |
| 1995 | Pat Summitt | Tennessee |
| 1996 | Leon Barmore | Louisiana Tech |
| 1997 | Geno Auriemma | Connecticut |
| 1998 | Pat Summitt | Tennessee |
| 1999 | Carolyn Peck | Purdue |
| 2000 | Geno Auriemma | Connecticut |

*Source: "Coach of the Year Award,"* Infoplease.com, *Learning Network, Inc., 2000. Available: http://In.infoplease.com/ipsa/A0003683.html, Voted on by the Women's Basketball Coaches Association and first presented by Converse athletic outfitters in 1983.*

**Lady Vols head coach Pat Summitt (University of Tennessee) is a three-time winner of the WCBA's prestigious Coach of the Year award.**

at last became the first woman ever to be inducted. Margaret Wade and Bertha F. Teague were also inducted.[5] In 2000, the Hall of Fame had inducted 14 women. (See Table 3.2)

In the spring of 1999, the Women's Basketball Hall of Fame enshrined its first class of 25. Earlier efforts to build a woman's

Table 3.2

## Women in the Naismith Basketball Hall of Fame Through 2000

| Name | Enshrined | School |
|---|---|---|
| Senda Berenson Abbott | Contributor, 1985 | Smith College (1892–1919) |
| Carol Blazejowski | Player, 1994 | Montclair State (1974–1978) |
| Jody Conradt | Coach, 1998 | U of Texas-Austin (1976– ) |
| Joan Crawford | Player, 1997 | Clarendon College (1955–1957) Nashville Business College (1957–1969) |
| Denise Curry | Player, 1997 | UCLA (1977–1981) |
| Anne Donovan | Player, 1995 | Old Dominion (1979–1983) |
| Nancy Lieberman-Cline | Player, 1996 | Old Dominion (1976–1980) |
| Ann Meyers | Player, 1993 | UCLA (1974–1978) |
| Cheryl Miller | Player, 1995 | USC (1993–1995) |
| Billie Moore | Coach, 1999 | Cal State, Fullerton (1969–1977) UCLA (1977–1993) |
| Uljana Semjonova | Player, 1993 | International Ball |
| Pat Head Summitt | Coach, 2000 | U of Tennessee (1974– ) |
| Bertha Teague | Contributor, 1985 | Byng High School, Ada, Oklahoma (1927–1969) |
| Margaret Wade | Coach, 1985 | Delta State (1973–1979) |

*Source: The Naismith Memorial Basketball Hall of Fame, Inc., 2000. Available: http://www.hoophall.com/halloffamers/year.htm.*

hall in Jackson, Tennessee, had been unsuccessful.[6] The Hall's inductees include Olympians Cheryl Miller, Nancy Lieberman-Cline, Ann Meyers-Drysdale and Pat Summitt, as well as early pioneers. (See Table 3.3.)

Basketball rules of play have changed, but so have the opportunities for women in the game. According to Nancy Lieberman-Cline,women now have the chance to display their skills to a wide audience for college and professional ball. "It has taken years for women to be able to play a game that we love with people in the stands and watching us on TV, with all of the trappings that have been afforded men's professional sports."[7] Lieberman-Cline says change has also taken place in both players and coaches. The biggest change, she says, is the increased depth and quality of the players. Title IX, scholarships, and televised games enable young

Tara VanDerveer of Stanford University, who was chosen as the WBCA Coach of the Year in 1989.

Table 3.3

# First Inductees to the Women's Basketball
# Hall of Fame, Spring 1999

| *Inductee* | *Contribution* |
|---|---|
| Senda Berenson Abbott | the mother of women's basketball, authored and developed the first basketball guide for women |
| Carol Blazejowski | prolific scorer, the first ever recipient of the Wade Trophy |
| Joanne Bracker | distinguished leader in the National Association of Intercollegiate Athletics (NAIA); compiled a .758 winning percentage during her 28-year career at Midland Lutheran College |
| Jody Conradt | the winningest coach in women's collegiate basketball history |
| Joan Crawford | 13-time AAU All-American |
| Denise Curry | two-time Olympian (1980 and 1984) and a three-time Kodak All-American at UCLA |
| Anne Donovan | three-time Olympian (1980, 1984, 1988) who set records that still stand at Old Dominion University |
| Carol Eckman | "Mother of National Collegiate Championships," established the first National Invitational Women's Intercollegiate Basketball Tournament in 1969 |
| Betty Jo Graber | established an early (possibly the first) women's basketball program in the Southwest |
| Luisa Harris Stewart | three-time Kodak All-American at Delta State University, scored the first points in Olympic women's basketball history as a member of the 1976 U.S. Olympic team |
| Nancy Lieberman-Cline | the only two-time winner of the Wade Trophy, became the youngest basketball player in Olympic history to win a medal at the age of 18 during the 1976 Olympics |
| Darlene May | internationally recognized as one of women's basketball all-time premier officials, became the first female to officiate an Olympic womens basket- |

**Table 3.3 (cont.)**

| *Inductee* | *Contribution* |
|---|---|
| | ball game at the 1984 games in Los Angeles |
| Ann Meyers-Drysdale | the first four-time Kodak All-American, was the first woman to receive a full athletic scholarship to UCLA |
| Cheryl Miller | led the University of Southern California to a 112–20 record and back-to-back NCAA titles in 1983 and 1984, and guided the United States to a gold medal in the 1984 Olympic Games |
| Billie Moore | holds the distinction of being the first USA Olympic Women's Basketball Coach, serving as head coach for the 1976 USA team |
| Pat Head Summitt | coached the USA to its first gold medal in women's basketball during the 1984 Olympics; has guided the University of Tennessee Lady Vols to six NCAA championships (1987, 1989, 1991, 1996, 1997 and 1998) |
| Margaret Wade | the Wade Trophy, given annually to the top women's collegiate player, is named in her honor |
| Nera White | a 15-time AAU All-American (1955-1969), tapped as the MVP at the AAU national tournament 10 times |

*Source: "Inaugural Class of Inductees Announced for Women's Basketball Hall of Fame," Business Wire (Knoxville), Nov. 15, 1998.*

---

girls to watch role models of what they can become. More opportunity, she says, brings more participation of talent. An example of that talent is a 6-foot-3 player who can play any position. Coaches "loosening up" is also a "huge change," says Lieberman-Cline. A wide-open style of basketball is being played, allowing players to express themselves.

## PLAYERS

Of the ten players the WNBA says "you should know," eight were active in the 1970s and or 1980s:

**Carol Blazejowski** holds the Madison Square Garden scoring record for both men and women with her 1978 52-point game for Montclair State against Queens College.

**Denise Curry,** two-time Olympian and three-time All America in the late 1970s, holds the University of California at Los Angeles (UCLA) record for most points logged, male or female, in a UCLA hoops career with 3,198. By 1999, Curry was the women's basketball head coach at California State at Fullerton.

**Anne Donovan** averaged a double-double at Old Dominion University (ODU) in 1979–1983, and led ODU to a 37–1 record and the Association for Intercollegiate Athletics for Women (AIAW) National Championship in her freshman season. She took ODU to the NCAA Final Four, was the first winner of the Naismith Player of the Year honors in 1983 and was a two-time Wade Trophy finalist. She played in three Olympics and became the head coach of the American Basketball League's Philadelphia Rage.

**Ann Meyers** is the first four-time women's basketball All-American, an honor she achieved while a UCLA Bruin. She was the first woman to be awarded a full athletic scholarship at UCLA. In 1978, she was designated the College Player of the Year and won the Broderick Cup when the Bruins won the national championship. She earned a silver medal in the Olympics. Meyers became a television commentator for college and professional ball.

**Uljana Semjonova,** center from Latvia, never lost in the 12 international games she played from 1970 through 1985, and earned 45 medals.

**Luisa Harris Stewart** in 1976 scored the first-ever basket in Olympic women's basketball. At Delta State she starred for Coach Margaret Wade (of Wade Trophy fame) on a three-time national championship team.[8]

Two additional players mentioned by the Women's National Basketball Association (WNBA) were Nancy Lieberman and Cheryl Miller. When women's basketball made its debut in 1976 at the Montreal Olympics, 18-year-old Nancy Lieberman became the youngest basketball player in Olympic history to win a medal when the United States won the silver.[9] Lieberman-Cline (who married former Continental Basketball Association player Tim Cline in 1987) is also the only player in the women's game to win the Wade Trophy twice, 1979 and 1980, and she was the first woman to play professional basketball with men (with the United States Basketball League's Springfield, Massachusetts, team). Lieberman-Cline served as general manager and head coach of the WNBA's Detroit Shock for three seasons, 1997–1999, earning a 46–48 record.

In 1984, Cheryl Miller led the United States in points, rebounds, assists and steals at the Los Angeles Olympics, when the women's team earned its first-ever gold medal. In high school, Miller was the first student—male or female—to be named a Parade All-American four years straight. At the University of Southern California, Miller was a four-time All-American, the only three-time Naismith Player of the year, a one-time Wade Trophy and Broderick Award winner. In 1983 and 1984, her team won two NCAA titles, and Miller earned honors three times as a member of the NCAA All-Tournament team and was twice the NCAA Tournament Most Valuable Player. She is the first athlete, male or female, to have her jersey retired at USC. She went on to become a Turner Network Television (TNT) sports commentator for the NBA games and the head coach of the WNBA's Phoenix Mercury.

An ESPN poll asked fans to name the "Number 1 Kodak All-American" of all time. The results overlapped the WNBA's "10 Players You Should Know" with Miller, Lieberman, Blazejowski, Donovan, Curry, Meyers and Harris. ESPN narrowed a list of players to 15 and asked users to rank them one through 15. Their ranked results are shown in Table 3.4.

In August 1999 USA Basketball announced the 1999–2000 Basketball Women's National Team: Ruthie Bolton-Holifield, guard, Sacramento; Cynthia Cooper, guard, Houston; Yolanda Griffith, Sacramento; Chamique Holdsclaw, forward, Washington; Lisa Leslie, forward-center, Los Angeles; Nikki McCray, guard, Washington; Delisha Milton, center, Los Angeles; Katie Smith, guard, Minnesota; Dawn Staley, guard, Charlotte; and Natalie Williams, forward, Utah. The squad includes five Olympic gold medalists, and nine of the ten have competed on at least one gold medal winning Olympic or world championship squad.[10]

## Organizations After 1972

The role of organizations in basketball is pivotal to giving women opportunity to compete and to providing society with an opportunity to see women compete. Many organization lines are drawn to this end. Some of the essential organizations are the

Table 3.4

## ESPN's Best Kodak All-American
## Basketball Players of All Time

| Rank | Player | Team | Year | Points |
|------|--------|------|------|--------|
| 1. | Chamique Holdsclaw | Tennessee | 1996–1998 | 57,240 |
| 2. | Cheryl Miller | University of Southern California | 1983–1986 | 44,622 |
| 3. | Sheryl Swoopes | Texas Tech | 1992–1993 | 40,060 |
| 4. | Teresa Edwards | Georgia | 1985–1986 | 36,171 |
| 5. | Nancy Lieberman | Old Dominion University | 1978–1980 | 31,389 |
| 6. | Carol Blazejowski | Montclair | 1976–1978 | 30,877 |
| 7. | Anne Donovan | Old Dominion University | 1981–1983 | 28,159 |
| 8. | Lisa Leslie | University of Southern California | 1994 | 27,548 |
| 9. | Denise Curry | University of California at Los Angeles | 1979–1981 | 26,586 |
| 10. | Ann Meyers | University of California at Los Angeles | 1975–1978 | 19,353 |
| 11. | Teresa Weatherspoon | Louisiana Tech | 1987–1988 | 18,417 |
| 12. | Luisa Harris | Delta State | 1975–1977 | 15,004 |
| 13. | Dawn Staley | Virginia | 1990–1992 | 14,475 |
| 14. | Lynette Woodard | Kansas | 1978–1981 | 11,774 |
| 15. | Pam Kelly | Louisiana Tech | 1980–1982 | 11,650 |

*Source: "The Best of All Time,"* Community, *ESPN.com Interact, March 25, 1999.*

Women's Basketball Coaches Association, the Association of Intercollegiate Athletics for Women, the National Collegiate Athletic Association, the American Basketball League, the Women's National Basketball Association, and the Women's Sport's Foundation.

WOMEN'S BASKETBALL COACHES ASSOCIATION (WBCA)

The WBCA was formed in 1981 "to promote women's basketball by unifying coaches at all levels to develop a reputable identity for the sport of women's basketball and to foster and promote the development of the game in all of its aspects as an amateur sport for women and girls."[11] It grew from about 212 members to over 5,000 members in 1999. The National Association of Basketball Coaches (NABC), WBCA's counterpart, was established in 1927.

## ASSOCIATION OF INTERCOLLEGIATE ATHLETICS FOR WOMEN (AIAW)

Founded in 1971, the AIAW was an early model for organizations promoting women's sports, and it gave women a voice in how their collegiate sports were structured according to Carpenter and Acosta. Once Title IX was in place, more women began participating in sports, and AIAW's membership and financial base grew; partly through its influence, women were involved in national governance of intercollegiate athletics. However, leadership positions previously held by women, such as coach, athletics director and sports official, soon came to be held by men. When the National Collegiate Athletic Association (NCAA) came on the scene of women's athletics, AIAW ultimately collapsed. The NCAA and the smaller National Association of Intercollegiate Athletics (NAIA) became the governing associations.

## NATIONAL COLLEGIATE ATHLETIC ASSOCIATION (NCAA)

For two decades, the NCAA resisted full implementation of Title IX, according to Deidre Duncan.[12] In 1992, the NCAA changed its focus, says Duncan, and established a Gender-Equity Task Force which issued a report. The NCAA revealed "that undergraduate enrollments were evenly divided by sex, but that men constituted 69.5 percent of the participants in intercollegiate athletics. The study also observed that men's programs received approximately 70 percent of the athletic scholarship funds, 77 percent of the operating budgets, and 83 percent of the recruiting money.[13] Sandy Keenan reports that "although women comprise roughly half of the students, women represent only 31 percent of the student athletes and receive an even lower percentage of the scholarship dollars."[14]

Darryl C. Wilson found in his research that the NCAA originated out of a perceived need to protect and preserve the amateur collegiate spirit and that this goal remains central to its expressed fundamental purposes. Monetary concerns, however, permeate the whole athletic system and play an integral part in what may at first appear to be very contradictory issues.

Wilson contends that for years, the NCAA has talked about participation as an issue of gender diversity, when in reality it is a budget issue. He adds however, that the two issues are related. Responding to the NCAA's 1997-98 budget based on revenues of $267 million, he says, "Serious issues arise regarding the NCAA's role as the distributor of these newfound millions and their response to the varying vulnerabilities of their members that fail to achieve equity."[15] The issues of conflict of interest lead one to ask whether the NCAA has lost sight of its original purpose, he says. "Huge" audiences and "large sums of money," appear to be causes.

### American Basketball League (ABL)

The ABL began its first season on October 18, 1996.[16] In 1995, Anne Cribbs, Steve Hams and Gary Cavalli, a public relations executive, formed the ABL. The league began to play in October 1996, but it faced competition the next summer when the National Basketball Association organized the Women's National Basketball Association (WNBA).[17] The ABL folded by the end of 1998, because of lack of funds, sponsorship and media exposure. The formation in 1997 of the WNBA contributed to ABL's collapse because the WNBA landed a national TV contract with NBC, NBA's partner, and got the benefits of a $15 million promotional effort by the NBA's marketing arm. *The Seattle Times* reported the ABL was not able to buy marketing time. Although ABL's attendance was improving, the WNBA's was better. The ABL may have had better talent, but they began losing players to the WNBA. In the end, ABL went bankrupt.[18]

The ABL is far from the first to falter. Six women's professional leagues were launched and tried to survive between 1976 (when women's basketball first became an Olympic event), and 1991, but failed.[19]

### Women's National Basketball Association (WNBA)

When the WNBA began on April 24, 1996, the NBA board of governors elevated women's basketball in America to the same level as men's.[20] Recruiting stars such as Theresa Edwards, Natalie

Williams, Jennifer Azzi, Katie Smith, Carolyn Jones Young and Yolanda Griffith from the ABL definitely benefitted the WNBA.[21] The WNBA played in the large stadiums in NBA cities while ABL played to mid-size audiences. The growth in media coverage on cable TV and the Internet have, in turn, contributed to the growth of women's professional leagues.

Betty Jaynes, the chief executive officer of the WBCA, served on USA Basketball's board of directors at the time of the WNBA's creation. "The NBA had been studying their league well over two years before the Olympics. They used the year before the Olympic games to see how the market would accept our national team. They traveled all over the country; did extremely well. Then when we won the Gold Medal in Atlanta, the WNBA went ahead and began to do their summer league."[22]

Packaging of women's sports at any level is critical not only to the success of the teams but also to the success of female coaches. The more successful female players are, whether in professional ball or high school athletics, the more successful the female coach will be in having full opportunity at all levels.

The NBA knew that female athletics could be marketed to male audiences. According to Daniel Green and Harris Collingwood, in 1997, on sales calls, NBA showed potential advertisers the research on what they called "the five powerful niche markets" for the WNBA:

1. the traditional sports fan: male, 18 to 49 years old, likes baseball, basketball, and football;
2. women 18 to 34 years old;
3. families with a daughter or other female relative who is active in competitive sports;
4. girls 7 to 17 who are looking for female sports role models;
5. boys 7 to 17 (surprising as it may seem, [Gary] Stevenson's [President NBA properties marketing and media group] research shows that many boys in this age group admire the high-intensity competition in women's basketball).

Advertisers not only use women for role models but also because they believe that "women are the next great market for sporting equipment."

The organization of the WNBA has contributed to the growth of women's basketball, but the growth brings challenge to the college scene. Some student athletes consider collegiate basketball an avenue to professional ball, but only a small number of elite players go on to pro ball. How do college coaches and athletic administrators see their role? Most see academics as the number one priority for the student athlete. Does the advent of the WNBA change the priority in the minds of student athletes?

Gail Goestenkors, coach at Duke University, says that although the WNBA has given basketball high visibility, a possible negative

Gail Goestenkors, head women's basketball coach at Duke University.

side effect is the increased emphasis on playing professional ball. "At times, players' education has taken a back seat, and I don't like that. That worries me, because very similar to the men, not many people actually get drafted. In that last draft, there were 11 seniors drafted, only 11. Two got cut. So only 9 seniors made teams. Only one of those seniors is starting and that is Chamique Holdsclaw. So, I'm going into homes this year, telling them those facts and figures. I don't want us to get to the point where academics takes a back seat."[23]

Iowa's Christine H. B. Grant believes advising student athletes about professional ball should begin on the junior high level. "Young student athletes need to know the odds. Fewer than one percent of the college athletes go into the pros. That means more than 99 percent never make it. Now does anyone sit down with a 14 year old and explain this? Because a 14 year old can be very intelligent. Would anybody buck these odds? There's nothing wrong with aspiring to be whatever, but you've got to be realistic. The realistic element doesn't seem to be getting through." It is normal, says Grant, for parents of talented athletes to dream about some of the huge salaries that the pros sign for. "It is the American dream, but probably the greatest disservice that we could ever do to a youngster is to feed that dream, because it's not going to happen. If the family feeds into the dream, the youngster then thinks, 'O.K., this is my shot. What's going to be my top priority?' Guess what's going to be her top priority. The whole system is so wrong."[24]

Tony DiCecco, the head women's basketball coach at the University of Northern Iowa, says that college is the teaching level. Student athletes come to college to get an education. And although the purpose for students and coaches is not to take care of the NBA, he believes that the WNBA and intercollegiate athletics are working together. DiCecco believes that the biggest recent change in the college game is in its direction.

> If it is marketed correctly, and we give the opportunity to those athletes that have the chance to develop their skills, we will see another explosion of women's basketball—because the talent is going to get better—and thus a need for more teams. You take a look at how pro sports have developed. You take a look at baseball, you take a

look at the NBA, you look at the NFL, as better players were coming out of college. Teams could have only so many people, and there was a need to put more players and more teams in professional sports. The same thing will happen with women's basketball.

We have to admit it's a business. People that have money want to invest in things that are going to make them money. There's no question right now that women's basketball is a very hot topic. A hot idea in terms of the businessperson who wants to pursue their dreams. A chance to make a lot of money.

DiCecco believes that college gives the student athlete a great opportunity to grow and become a young man or a young woman, and there are some steps during college that should not be skipped. "The WNBA is preaching the right thing: 'You gotta get through school.' I think that's good."

Jody Conradt, coach at the University of Texas, says she does not as yet hear many athletes saying, "Oh, I don't have to worry about getting a degree because I'm going to advance to the WNBA and make my fortune there"—but that doesn't mean that it won't happen. So far, says Conradt, "the salaries that players in the WNBA are drawing don't unbalance the scale toward making money over getting a college degree. Athletes want to get their degree, and then maybe later they will play professional ball. I can't guarantee that that philosophy will remain, but right now that's where we are."[25]

The WBCA's Betty Jaynes says that it is true that not all of our female players are going to get an opportunity to compete professionally. However, the biggest accomplishment of the WNBA is that it provides an opportunity for female players to compete when they will be at their peak of performance. Jaynes says, "This league is for the highly skilled, but in the WNBA's embryonic stages, probably more players are going to get a chance to play, because the pool isn't huge as it is in the men's game yet. So, the potential league member graduating in 2000 from college might have a better shot at a WNBA career than the 2010 class. It's just a growth stage that we're in."[26] Jaynes says that the WNBA has "tremendous effect on our college players because it does give them something else to reach for."

Some successful college coaches and players have moved on to coach professional basketball in the WNBA. Among them are

Carolyn Peck in her days as head coach of women's basketball at Purdue. Peck went on to become general manager and head coach of the WNBA's Orlando Miracle. (Photograph: Purdue DIS Photo.)

Carolyn Peck, the general manager and head coach of the Orlando Miracle, who won the 1999 NCAA tournament as coach of the Purdue Boilermakers. Nancy Lieberman-Cline, a three season coach of the Detroit Shock, was an outstanding player in college and professional ball. Cheryl Miller, general manager and coach of the Phoenix Mercury excelled as a college player and coach at the University of Southern California.

Bernadette McGlade, the assistant commissioner of the Atlantic Coast Conference, believes that the WNBA has accelerated the growth and the popularity of women's basketball because it has the resources necessary to support the league:

> It certainly has been a great catalyst that was well timed coming on the heels of the '96 Olympics in Atlanta and the popularity of the games. The NBA's structuring of the financial backing and the support to launch the league has certainly brought women's basketball to an extremely high degree into the homes of America. That is the one thing that the colleges and universities haven't been able to do. They haven't been able to do it because of not really having a

comprehensive television package. All of the work that coaches, administrators and players did during the development from the 1960s to the 1980s and into the 1990s helped the game grow in popularity, but the WNBA was really able to take advantage of that grass roots growth and turn the heat up by bringing it into every home in America.[27]

Donna Lopiano of the WSF points out a most positive effect of the WNBA: Sport-related careers are now available for women college basketball players. They can be professional athletes here in the United States. Before the WNBA, they had to go abroad in order to have access to that opportunity.[28]

Vivian Acosta agrees that the WNBA gives collegiate players the opportunity to extend their playing careers here in the United States. Thus players' skills will be recognized here, and women will be able to play in front of home teams or family in locales where they are known instead of in Europe where they are unknown.[29]

Inevitably, however, the WNBA contributes in some measure to the growing pains of women's basketball. Barbara Stevens at Bentley College in Waltham, Massachusetts, sees some pitfalls. "The vision of glory and money may change how individuals view their college years. They may see them as just a preparatory situation before they get into the professional ranks. The illusion that all good players go on to play professional sports is really a little deceiving to young students." Stevens concedes that the WNBA has brought name recognition to the sport of women's basketball. But when a product is on TV, and the young people watch it, they want to emulate the people they see on TV. The role models have a great impact. "I would like to see it remain a positive impact," says Stevens.

> This is where we tread a little bit on dangerous waters because TV can have a negative impact. We've seen it in some professional sports where messages are sent by the athletes' behavior or method of responding to certain situations where it's not positive. I would hope that the WNBA players, coaches, and administrators can keep the game positive for female athletes, and make it a situation where young people will receive a good message, an encouraging message, as opposed to one of acting out in a manner that is inappropriate.[30]

Perhaps the WNBA's arrival and the resulting growth to women's basketball are, as Stevens says, " a sign of the times, and necessary for the sport to grow. You've also seen some growing pains as well. There are things happening in our sport as a result of just the growth that is occurring. Some are good and some are not so good."

WOMEN'S SPORTS FOUNDATION (WSF)

Billie Jean King established the WSF in 1974 as a national non-profit organization. Their noble mission is "to promote lifelong participation and growth of females in sports and fitness."[31] It is "dedicated to increasing opportunities for girls and women in sports and fitness through education, advocacy, recognition and grants.... The Foundation seeks to create an educated public that encourages females' participation and supports gender equality in sport."

## The Role of Participant Recruitment

A good coach knows that in order to have a top winning team, she has to recruit top quality players. The ability to recruit those players depends, in part, on the availability of funding. But the importance of a quality player cannot be overestimated. Pat Summitt of the University of Tennessee understood player importance at times of loss and at times of winning. Success is putting the right people in the right place at the right time. Summitt says, "Team building starts by recruiting good people and turning them into willing role players early on."[32] Summitt's 1997-98 undefeated season inspired another book, *Raise the Roof*, to tell the remarkable story of her team, the Lady Vols—a team so good that they changed her coaching style to one of giving the team the control.[33]

Another reason to recruit good players, says Grace-Marie Mowery, is that a greater number of top quality female athletes should create a larger pool of potential female coaches.[34] Some researchers say that it should create a larger pool of qualified coaches for both genders. Whatever the gender of the coach hired, recruitment of the participant remains critical. In some cases, how much participant recruiting is required of a coach and whether a team wins or loses determine the coach's pay.

Pat Summitt of the University of Tennessee. (Photograph: The Photography Center, University of Tennessee.)

## The Role of Women in High School Basketball, Players and Coaches, a Pipeline

*"Hell hath no fury like the parent of an athletic daughter scorned."*[35]

Gender-equity in high school athletics, say Ray Yasser and Samuel J. Schiller, is the new frontier, even though the struggle on the collegiate level is not over. Unless younger girls can participate fully in interscholastic sports, participation on the college level is both problematical and theoretical. Michael Straubel states that discrimination at the high school and junior high school levels may be causing more men than women to participate in athletics at the college level. The result is, nevertheless, that women are not taking advantage of the opportunities to participate at the same rate as men.[36] According to Straubel, a 1996 survey by the NCAA supports this conclusion.[37] Straubel argues that most sports played at the college level are played at the high school level; if they are not, they usually cannot survive. It is not likely a particular sport will be played for the first time at the college level. The school must set its anchor in "safe harbor," says Straubel. In order to get the 12 year old participant who becomes the high school participant and then the college participant, nonmedia "grassroots" athletics are needed. Generating a critical mass at the lower, younger levels will sustain college teams. Straubel concludes that women's interest in athletics must be created and nurtured in the high schools and the middle schools. Proportionality by males and females has to be a reality in the high schools before it can be so in colleges.[38]

As we give more opportunity to girls and women in school athletic programs, we expand the horizons of both the woman athletic participant and the woman coach. As we lift the barriers (of funding, societal perceptions, or whatever they may be), we insure greater participation for men and women alike at all educational levels and in all athletic programs.

Donna Lopiano's 1999 research found, in general, that our schools have made progress in meeting the requirements of Title IX. She found in high schools that the participation of both boy and girl athletes has increased, but that boys comprise 60 percent and girls 40 percent of the participants.[39] The 1999 High School Athletics Participation Survey found basketball to be the most popular of the sports programs for girls, with 456,873 participants and 16,439 school programs.[40]

The opportunity to participate on the high school level translates into our middle and elementary school students having a ball in their hands, says Nancy Hoppe, post forward on a 6-on-6 team at Reinbeck High School, Reinbeck, Iowa, in the 1950s.

When AAU [Amateur Athletic Union] ball came into being—that's when they started playing basketball, I'd say, in the fourth grade. It's important that you get parents who are interested and who are willing to work with kids at that level to develop their skills way back then.... I think we had one of the better basketball programs in the state for maybe the last six to eight years. We had a good coach who got kids to go on to State [tournaments], and another reason for the kids going to State is that we have good parents and kids have played since a young age. They handle the basketball and they know what to do with it. It's also become common, in this area at least, with West Waterloo and Cedar Falls being quality basketball programs, that we get coaches in our audience often. Pat Summitt [University of Tennessee] has been here a number of times. Angie Lee, women's head coach of the University of Iowa, has been here a number of times, and of course, our UNI coach, Tony DiCecco, comes to a lot of our games as his schedule permits.[41]

Not only are players developed in the lower grades; coaches are as well. "Coaches are getting better and better," Duke's Gail Goestenkors says.[42] The reason, she says, is that nowadays the younger coaches played girls' basketball from third, fourth, or fifth grade up. As a result, some women are now as qualified as or more qualified than men. In earlier decades, only men had organized basketball and the chance to play early in life to develop that feel for the game. Now, men and women are on even playing ground, as more and more qualified women are coming up through the ranks.

### High School Coaches

Not only does the opportunity to participate in high school athletics increase the opportunity to do so at the college level; it also increases the chance that some of those participants may become high school coaches. High school coaches might later become college coaches, and college coaches often become coaches of professional teams. The interrelationship of the levels is critical to all.

## The Role of Professional Ball

Money is a big part of professional ball. College players cannot accept money, but the same elements are at work. In 1997, for example, Nike, Kodak, and Reebok sponsored the NCAA women's basketball Final Four in Cincinnati.[43] (Final Four is the playoff round for the top four teams out of 64 that have gone through the NCAA basketball tournament.) The fan base grows, tickets sell out, and media ratings go up. The reality of professional basketball in relationship to collegiate basketball is that only the very elite will participate. In addition, the goal of collegiate basketball is to aid its student athletes to obtain an academic degree to prepare them for life. The goal of professional basketball is to play for monetary compensation.

## The Role of the Olympics

Donna A. Lopiano says, "We cannot look at the role of women in sport without an understanding of the larger society in which sport resides."[44] She believes that when women are given an opportunity to participate, their achievements will eliminate the barriers. Lopiano's philosophy can be applied to the college woman coach. As the larger society is given opportunities to see her perform, the walls will begin to fall.

Perhaps nowhere are economic forces as strong as in the global marketplace. "Even nations that disapprove of female participation in sport will rally around the idiosyncratic Olympic champion," says Lopiano. Sports help nations transcend dividing lines. Economies lag when nations use only half their talent; thus, she says, "the female athlete will come of age" around the world.

In the United States, Lopiano's philosophy echoes scholars Ray Yasser and Samuel J. Schiller, who say that today's fathers of athletic daughters have "inexorably changed the nature of the battle for sports resources."[45] Thus, at the Olympic level, says Lopiano, the real question is not "whether" but "when?"

In 1992, Curry Kirkpatrick characterized Olympian basketball performances this way: "After all, it's not the U.S. men who have earned gold medals in two consecutive Olympics and have won 45 of their last 47 games in international competition while saving Uncle Sam's reputation on the court."[46]

In 1997, Theresa Edwards, a two-time Olympian, both coached and played for the Atlanta Glory, a team in the now defunct American Basketball League.[47]

## An Epoch of Eyewitnesses

Women's basketball has indeed grown in the last two decades, and convincing evidence suggests that attendance is increasing. In

1997-98, the NCAA's women's national home basketball attendance "reached an all-time high" as it "cruised past the seven million mark for the first time."[48] A total of 7,387,355 fans attended all NCAA women's varsity basketball games, a net increase of 653,194 (9.7 percent) over the 1996-97 total. Attendance increased at every level. For 1998-99, attendance passed the eight million mark at 8,010,227. (See Table 3.5.)

The NCAA says that no matter what "measuring stick" is used, the 1999 Division I Women's Basketball Championship had spectator appeal. The title game between Purdue University and Duke University drew a ESPN record television rating of 4.3, an average of 3.238 million viewers, the second-largest audience for a men's

Table 3.5

## NCAA Women's Basketball Attendance History(Includes NCAA Home, Tournament and Neutral Sites)

| Year | Teams | All NCAA Divisions Attendance | P/G* Avg. | Change in Avg. | |
|------|-------|------------|-----------|-------|----|
| 1982 | 764 | 1,926,989 | 281 | — | |
| 1983 | 764 | 2,429,461 | 331 | Up | 50 |
| 1984 | 749 | 2,251,014 | 355 | Up | 24 |
| 1985 | 746 | 2,309,469 | 354 | Dn | 1 |
| 1986 | 760 | 2,348,729 | 348 | Dn | 6 |
| 1987 | 756 | 2,439,877 | 366 | Up | 18 |
| 1988 | 754 | 2,649,079 | 397 | Up | 31 |
| 1989 | 765 | 2,866,898 | 426 | Up | 29 |
| 1990 | 782 | 3,183,871 | 463 | Up | 37 |
| 1991 | 806 | 3,407,247 | 459 | Dn | 4 |
| 1992 | 815 | 3,827,711 | 536 | Up | 77 |
| 1993 | 894 | 4,193,243 | 600 | Up | 64 |
| 1994 | 859 | 4,557,066 | 642 | Up | 42 |
| 1995 | 864 | 4,961,946 | 679 | Up | 37 |
| 1996 | 874 | 5,233,954 | 703 | Up | 24 |
| 1997 | 879 | 6,734,141 | 675 | Dn | 28 |
| 1998 | 911 | 7,387,335 | 692 | Up | 17 |
| 1999 | 940 | 8,010,227 | 715 | Up | 23 |

Source: Rick Campbell, fax to author, Nov. 22, 1999.
*Persons per Game.
Note: Beginning in 1997, home attendance included double-headers with men in which separate attendance was taken by halftime of the women's game.

or women's basketball game on ESPN.[49] Clearly, attendance and ratings indicate increased growth for women's basketball.

It appears that basketball has transcended gender, race and terminology and has become one of the world's most popular sports.[50]

# Chapter 4

# *Contributors to the Game: Selected Profiles*

*"If the concern is to remain for student athletes, we should be trying to reform."*

Christine H. B. Grant
Athletic Director for Women
University of Iowa[1]

Athletic administrators and other professionals have contributed to women's basketball. Many good athletic administrators and athletic organizational officials have made a difference for the women's game. Profiling some very able women administrators helps us to see the intricate interrelationship of administration and the game of basketball. Dr. Donna A. Lopiano, the executive director of the Women's Sports Foundation, has been a diligent advocate of equity for women in sports. Betty Jaynes, chief executive officer for the Women's Basketball Coaches Association, gives sensible perspective, and predicts that basketball's growth in the new millennium will exceed its present point. Christine H. B. Grant, athletic director for Women at the University of Iowa since 1973, shares both realistic and idealistic philosophy. Bernadette V. McGlade is the first-ever assistant commissioner of Women's Basketball Operations for the Atlantic Coast Conference. Sue Rodin founded Women in Sports and Events (WISE) as a national networking organization for female executives.

Two scholars in the field of sport give us a look at their philosophies. R. Vivian Acosta and Linda Jean Carpenter have conducted an important longitudinal study of women in intercollegiate sport, analyzing the changes that have taken place over a 21 year period. The study has had an impact both within and outside the profession.

The number of male coaches of women's basketball is increasing. Among the many men who have contributed to women's basketball as head coaches are Geno Auriemma from the University of Connecticut, who coached the UConn team to the 1995 NCAA national championship; Leon Barmore from Louisiana Tech, whose Lady Techsters won the 1988 NCAA championship; and Tony DiCecco of the University of Northern Iowa, who has turned the women's program toward a winning tradition.

# Academicians, Administrators and Organization Professionals

## R. Vivian Acosta[2]

Vivian Acosta, a professor in theDepartment of Physical Education and Exercise Science at Brooklyn College, Brooklyn, New York, says she is "a normal, every day kind of coach," and finds that the continuation of association with former players the greatest satisfaction of her coaching career. "We have become very good friends and have followed each other's careers," she says.

Acosta made one of her most significant contributions to her college basketball program when AIAW was in existence. She was the tournament director of the regional tournament held at Brooklyn College. "The tournament went very, very well. We had many obstacles to overcome, but it was a good tournament and I think people enjoyed it very much."

Acosta played as a forward in the 1950s and has seen 40 years of change in basketball. "When we went to the five player game, I continued to really enjoy that kind of game. The kinds of defenses and offenses have changed over the years. The game has really evolved so that it is no longer a game that is played by, as we were referred to, little girls who can't run the full court, and don't have the skill to do that or the endurance to do a game where it is fully, fully enjoyed by women players."

Acosta says that as a player she valued the opportunity to play different kinds of sports. "It opened doors for me that I would not have not had. When I entered college, I started playing field hockey. I had no previous experience with field hockey. That opened doors to me that were wonderful. It also showed me that I was a good player because I was selected to play on all-star teams and selected teams." But, she adds, when she became a coach and entered her profes-

R. Vivian Acosta, professor emerita, Brooklyn College. (Photograph: Richard Barnes.)

sional career, she began to wonder "what could have been for me as a player in any sport if I had had the opportunity to develop my athletic skills and talent to the fullest of my ability by focusing on a particular sport as is done nowadays. So, that I regret, because I'll never know how far I could have gone."

When she was a player in college, practice sessions were limited to a week or two, and there were no regional competitions or national championship games. "We had sports days and play days where we went to another school and played games, and that was it. The seasons just didn't exist. They were very, very short," she says.

Acosta says she never questioned playing on a half court, but then she started playing full court: "I thought, 'Why haven't we been doing this all along? This is so much fun and it's so much better.'" With the change to full court, women athletes were able to develop both their guarding and shooting skills and became all around players rather than being limited to a specialized position. Acosta says that the changes the game has undergone also contribute to the progress. Women's basketball is now "real" basketball.

Acosta has seen a lot of significant changes in the coaching profession. When she was a player in college, the coaches were volunteers. They were physical educators. Volunteers no longer exist on the collegiate or high school level. Coaches are now full-time, and have to be really knowledgeable about the sport. They have become specialists. There is more intensity in the role of the coach, especially because the coach's job and future may depend on her win-loss record.

Acosta earned her Ph.D. from the University of Southern California in 1974. From 1965 to 1967 she coached women's field hockey and volleyball at Brigham Young University. From 1967 to 1980, she coached women's basketball and softball and men's and women's badminton. She was a Region One section coach for the United States Badminton Association, a special clinician for the Guatemala National Badminton Team, and a participant in the Pan American Coaches Clinic for the International Badminton Federation. Among her numerous athletic positions she has served as women's athletic director at Brooklyn College from 1969 to 1974. Since 1995, she has served as the college's senior associate athletic director and senior woman administrator. She has written over 15 scholarly works, several book chapters and three books on girls and women in athletics.

Acosta has appreciated the impact of sports in her own life. She says, "Sport in itself has offered me a life long opportunity to affiliate with people who enjoy life, who are upbeat, and who are positive in their outlook. It has also provided me with long lasting and valued friendships. All of my really good friends come out of sports. Sport has also provided me with a wonderful career, as a teacher, a coach and an athletic administrator. Sport is a profession where I've made a difference in people's lives, and that to me is important."

### LINDA JEAN CARPENTER[3]

What was, or is, the impact of Title IX on women's college basketball programs? Linda Carpenter, professor at Brooklyn College, Brooklyn, New York, and an attorney at law, says:

Athletes don't have to play in the "women's gym" anymore.... Title IX has had a great impact on all of basketball's support systems: facilities, equipment, uniforms. It has benefitted basketball the most of any of the sports, because basketball is a sport that the guys can relate to a little better than some of the other women's sports. So, when there has been increased support at the best, Title IX has been filtered into basketball much more readily than field hockey or volleyball which are historically the women's sports in the United States. It has made basketball a major sport for women,

Linda Jean Carpenter, professor emerita, Brooklyn College. (Photograph: George Bing.)

thus basketball has gotten the lion's share of the support as well. That's had an effect on the coaches' salaries of the women's teams, too. Although they are still lagging far behind the men's teams, they are greatly ahead of the minor sports' coaching salaries. Title IX and the informal designation as a major sport have increased the number of colleges that offer basketball for women. Approximately 98 per cent of the schools offer women's basketball.

When Carpenter started playing there were three positions: guard, center and forward. Carpenter says that she was a good guard, but she was frustrated when the game progressed:

> I hated being a rover because no one had ever taught me the skills you needed to be a forward. When it was my turn to be on that end of the court, if I got the ball, I was good at rebounding and picking up the ball but I had no clue what to do with it. The game now

has progressed greatly, but the game then, pre–Title IX, limited skill development.

The coaches were volunteers. They were physical educators who were willing to give extra hours to coach most often rather than being paid. There was no money to support travel to other schools, much less buy uniforms, shoes, lunch, hotel rooms, and anything else. So that cut down on the competition, as did the notion in our day that women should not be engaged in heavy duty competition.

Title IX would not have been enacted 10 years before it was, because society wasn't ready to see women having full opportunities, says Carpenter:

> When we were in college, we could be assertive, pushy and shovey on the basketball court, but we had to go into the locker room and change into frilly blouses and skirts. That we would leave in pants or warmup suits was against the rules. Society's maturation and ability to see the value of women has also had an effect on seeing women be assertive, be sweaty, be pushy, shovey; the things on the basketball court seem to be okay for women to be actually doing. That's maturation. More begets more, so when you've had women who have had good experiences on the basketball court as well as in the other activities, they want more for their daughters and are willing to support their daughters.

Today, Carpenter says, enforcement of Title IX especially in the most visible sport, basketball, is becoming more equitable. She asks, "Have women sports arrived to where there is no need to enforce Title IX anymore? No." She believes that the greatest inequity is in salaries. To correct those inequities would require considerable enforcement of Title IX and other rules. The EEOC's, 1997 *Guidance* on enforcing Title VII and the Equal Pay Act for coaches' salaries spelled out some of the excuses that are used for not paying women equally for their work. Carpenter says that because the *Guidance* was so well written, it has given the coaches a new sense of their own worth: "It's time for me to be treated equally. I've been fighting for my students to be treated equally; now it's time for me. Maybe this is some help for me," coaches say.

According to Carpenter the obstacles that could prevent women's programs from reaching equity with men's are "strictly a matter of will." She points out that especially coaches of women's teams tend to hold one-year appointments, and to be kept at one-year appointments, which is an effective way of keeping their salaries and status low:

> Keeping coaches on temporary appointments makes it difficult for those coaches to be the focus of the enforcement push. But as women realize that and are speaking for multiple year contracts, and as the Office for Civil Rights of the U.S. Department of Education continues to try to better enforce Title IX and the Justice Department and the EEOC try, I think that will help. Parents of girls in high school are understanding that they are the greatest force in enforcement and are exercising their rights for their daughters to rattle cages and file complaints more frequently. So, I don't think there are any barriers to total enforcement. I know some people are shaking in their boots that Congress might repeal Title IX. It's not going to happen. I can't imagine that somebody would get reelected very quickly if you could say that Congressman Smith voted to remove federal legislation that guaranteed equity for women in the educational program. The issues have been litigated. There is nothing left to argue about with the regulations. People will continue arguing, but there's nothing left to argue.

Carpenter says that in the last decade most court decisions favor compliance with and enforcement of gender equity regulations. In other words, the women are winning. Athletic directors, the majority of whom are men, are making wiser decisions. "They are no longer fighting and struggling against the enforcement of the law, but have decided to put their money into their programs instead of into lawyers' hands to fight the position of the law or the enforcement of the law." Carpenter concedes that some unenlightened decision making remains, but that real support exists for gender equity in sports.

> More and more people want to be part of the solution instead of part of the problem. Some may not know how to be part of the solution totally, because it is difficult. It has been 29 years since Title IX has been enacted, and it is difficult to comply if you haven't been complying all along. It is going to cost the institution a lot of money. If they have been complying all along, there is no problem. But those institutions that have not been following Title IX's guidelines are really struggling to find ways to do so now. But as a group, those institutions are sharing information now about how to do it instead of sharing information on how to fight it. That's a big difference.

The only remaining struggle, if there is one, is when schools, rather than take any money away from the rich football programs, decide to cut men's minor sports in order to find money to meet their gender equity requirements. Cutting the men's teams is an intolerable decision on the part of the administrators. And still there are institutions that have decided not to cut anything from their men's football teams, including nights at a hotel before home games; this money would fund the men's minor sports for a good long time. So, I think that's the last remaining issue.

Carpenter earned her Ph.D. from the University of California in 1974 and her J.D. degree from Fordham University School of Law in 1981. She is also a member of the New York State Bar and the United States Supreme Court Bar. She has served on a variety of national committees and currently serves on the Women in Sports Committee of the United States Olympic Committee and committees for the Women's Sports Foundation. She has authored five scholarly books, including four on girls and women in sports. She has written 10 book chapters and more than 30 articles for scholarly journals.

Carpenter says there is no doubt that sport belongs on campus:

> I'm afraid that we will do to sport things which will make people doubt its value. It is a laboratory wherein both men and women learn life skills. Students learn about themselves, learn about risk evaluation, learn about courage, learn about team work, learn all those things. And if sports are not present on campus or if they continue to move toward less than admirable enterprises, if they're allowed to seek their lowest common denominator, what a loss for both men and women. Sport is empowering to both men and women because it lets them learn skills that they cannot learn anywhere else on campus or in today's society.

### CHRISTINE H. B. GRANT[4]

"The main factor that has contributed to the progress in the growth of all women's sports is Title IX," says Dr. Christine Grant.

> When you look, you see, yes, we've come a long way. There's no question, no question at all. But it's now 29 years since Title IX was passed, and we still have a long, long way to go. Yet, if anybody asked me, "Would we have seen this kind of progress without

Title IX?" I would answer, "Absolutely not!" They've had 29 years to get to where we should be and we're still not there. You're going to tell me that we are going to voluntarily do it? Dream on! No way! No, it will not be done voluntarily, unfortunately.

Grant, who has had a long and distinguished career in the administration of athletics, began her career in coaching. From 1956 to 1961 she coached field hockey, netball and track at Graeme High School and Lindsay High School in Scotland. In 1961–1964 she coached basketball, field hockey

**Christine Grant, athletic director for women, University of Iowa.**

and track at Burnaby High School in British Columbia, and she did so again in 1964-1965 at Brookfield High School, Ottawa Canada. In 1963 she was the national coach of the Canadian Women's Field Hockey Team in the International Conference and Tournament at Baltimore, Maryland. In 1965, she instigated and organized the first Canadian national field hockey tournament. From 1965 to 1971, she coached basketball, track and field at East York Collegiate, Toronto, Canada. In 1970 Grant received the Ontario Sports Award for Outstanding Contributions to Canadian Amateur Sport.

In her position at the University of Iowa, she has guided the women's program to national prominence. Among Grant's numerous prestigious and pertinent appointments is her service, in 1973-1974, as a member of AIAW Athletic Directors' Workshop Committee which organized the first AIAW National Workshop on the Administration of Women's Intercollegiate Athletic Programs.

In 1975-1976, she was a member of the joint AIAW-NCAA Committee to explore compatibility of their policies. In 1977 she was a member of Council of Ten Special Committee to study the role of women in the Big Ten Conference.

In 1979, she served as a panelist on the MacNeil-Lehrer Report, "Title IX," in Chicago, Illinois, and she was a panelist at the tenth National Conference on Women in Law, "Title IX," in San Antonio, Texas. From 1980 to 1981, she served as president of the AIAW. In 1987–1989, she was president of the National Association of Collegiate Women Athletic Administrators. In 1988–1990, she served on the NCAA Special Committee to Review the NCAA Membership Structure.

From 1985 to 1995 she served as chair of the National Wade Trophy Committee, whose function was to select the nation's outstanding basketball scholar-athlete. In 1994–1997, she was the NACWAA chair of the Committee on Gender Equity.

In 1999, she continued as an ethics fellow, International Institute for Sport; she serves on the NCAA cabinet for Academics, Eligibility, and Compliance, as well as the chair of Subcommittee on Amateurism and Agents.

Among Grant's many honors, in 1978 she was named in *Who's Who of American Women*. In 1988, she received the Presidential Award in recognition of outstanding contributions to girls and women in sport from the National Association for Girls and Women in Sport. In 1995, she received the Billie Jean King Contribution Award from the Women's Sports Foundation. In 1992, she was the co-recipient of the first Lou Henry Hoover Award for outstanding contributions to development of girls' and women's sports in Iowa, and the Women's Basketball Coaches Association National Administrator of the Year Award. In 1993, she was named to the World Who's Who of Women, and received the NACWAA National Administrator of the Year Award. In 1994, she was inducted into the Hall of Fame of the Women's Institute on Sport and Education. In 1998, she received the NCAA Honda Award of Merit for Outstanding Achievement in Women's Collegiate Athletics.

On more than twenty occasions she has testified in behalf of Title IX, including, in 1978-1979, to the HEW Office for Civil Rights Task Force and in 1979, before the U.S. Commission on Civil Rights. In 1998 she was selected to speak before the U.S. Senate Judiciary Committee.

Grant says that when she speaks about the entire women's intercollegiate athletic scene, she is also speaking about the basketball situation. She offers valuable historical background of "blatant" but unacknowledged discrimination. In 1972, when Title IX was passed, about 8 percent of the high school athletes were female. "So, that meant 92 percent were male." Grant points out, "Now at the high school level, 40 percent are female and 60 percent male. The same type of explosion occurred at the intercollegiate level." Grant says figures are not exact, but there were very few real varsity programs for women in the early 1970s. They just did not exist. Programs existed as club sports. "Students had to pay for the opportunity to participate, which was really ironic because the same female students were paying tuition and fees to the universities, and the universities in many instances were funding the men's intercollegiate varsity programs. So the women, actually, were subsidizing the men and then having to turn around and dip twice into their own pocket—if they wanted even to experience club sports, not varsity, just club."

The 1980s were years without much progress regarding Title IX, but Grant says that in 1992, progress accelerated because people were willing to take legal action. The present accelerated growth results from many factors. Parents are getting more into the scene because sports can provide access to scholarships to higher education, especially at the Division I and II levels. Schools are interested in building successful programs that bring the large crowds—and thus dollars. The NCAA data for the last five or six years demonstrate attendance figures are going up and up. Women's collegiate sport is still all about women creating a fan base that's composed of everybody from five to eighty-five years old. It's a family affair, a different approach to sports.

There is more than one problem in the pay scale, says Grant. "I don't agree with the model of the basketball coach being paid several times as much as the next coach who may be way better than she is or he is. If the concern is to remain for student athletes, we should be trying to reform. In the spring of 1999, the NCAA appointed a special committee to reform men's basketball. Women's basketball should not duplicate a major salary inequity problem that is in men's basketball."

Grant's focus in on the student athlete. She maintains that in order to help that athlete, intercollegiate athletics needs to undergo reform, and that reform would include correcting inequity in coaching salaries as well as other expenditures due to overcommercialization. She opposes Division I's trend toward spending more and more and more money on fewer and fewer student athletes:

> We've created a system and entrapped ourselves into following a professional model. We're going to have to get ourselves out of this trap, because we are not professional sport. We must never aspire to be professionals. Intercollegiate programs can be justified in our universities; I can't justify pro sport in the university. I cannot philosophically do it. We offer intercollegiate not to fill the stadiums, but to create successful individuals. Fans are a byproduct. The real product is a poised, articulate, highly successful, and great human being,– that's success.
>
> I would very much like to see a Blue Ribbon Committee of NCAA presidents and then some of best minds on the athletic scene sit down and reform intercollegiate athletics for this century. We are spiraling totally out of control financially, especially in Division I, in order to pay the enormous compensation packages. The facilities race is such that as soon as the building is built, you go to the end of the pack again and you've got to keep up this arms race. We've got to reform it. Totally and utterly reform it. Women have obviously got to be in there, because they have some ideas on how to set about it.

### BETTY F. JAYNES[5]

Betty F. Jaynes of the WBCA says that women's basketball is a great game:

> But you haven't seen anything yet. This is the comparison for women's basketball in 1999: If you looked at a house that had just a foundation–that's what we've got. We don't have any walls up. We don't have a roof. We don't have any furniture in the house. That's how the game and the intensity of the game and the quality of the game is going to change in the next millennium. So what you will see in 2010, you might have the sides of the house up and maybe the roof on, but that is the state of the game. It is very embryonic. We've got the ability to do it. We've got the coaches to do it. We've got the training facilities to do it. We've got the athletes coming up through the grade schools that will make a big difference. That will happen in 2010. We don't want to live and accept the way our college and high school game is right now.

Jaynes has been a leader in women's basketball for over 25 years. In 1996, she was named the WBCA's chief executive officer after serving 15 years as its executive director. WBCA was founded in 1981, and has grown under her leadership from its beginning of 212 members to over 5,000 members.

As CEO, Jaynes is the organization's chief liaison to affiliated governing bodies and sport organizations. In addition, she oversees its legislative role with the NCAA and handles additional advisory affairs as necessary. Jaynes says that one of her greatest satisfactions is having been asked to be in a leadership role in WBCA. Her tasks are many: to work with coaches; to make it clear that the WBCA is a professional endeavor; and to provide a forum.

Betty Jaynes, chief executive officer, Women's Basketball Coaches Association.

Among Jaynes' many national honors are seats on the Women's Basketball Hall of Fame board of directors and the Atlanta Tip-Off Club board of directors (vice president 1992–1999). She is a Naismith Memorial Basketball Hall of Fame trustee; she sits on the Naismith Memorial Basketball Hall of Fame Executive Committee and is the Women's Screening Committee chair; she is a member of the USA Basketball board of directors and chair of its By-Laws Committee; and she also sits on the Center of the Study of Sport in Society National Advisory Committee. She is a Women's Sports Foundation trustee and has been co-chair of its Coaches Council. In 1991 and 1997 she received the President's Award from the WBCA. In 1995, she received the NACDA Honors Award and was inducted into the Communiplex Women's Sports Hall of Fame.

Jaynes lettered in basketball in the position of stationary guard for four years at Newton County High School, Georgia. She was named an all-state player in her junior and senior years. In her senior year, her team had a 33–1 record and earned a berth in the 1963 Class AA state championship game in Atlanta. She earned her B.S. degree in physical education from Georgia College in 1976. She received her master's degree from the University of North Carolina at Greensboro in 1968. From 1970 to 1982 Jaynes served as head women's basketball coach at Madison College (now renamed James Madison College), where she led her team to a 142–114 record. In 1975, her team won the Association for Intercollegiate Athletics for Women(AIAW) state championship. In 1973, 1977, and 1979 her teams posted runner-up finishes. In 1978-79 her team earned the first 20-win season in school history at 20-7. In 1974 and 1975 her teams advanced to the AIAW Region 2 playoffs.

As a coach, Jaynes was exposed to the five-player game. She says that the changes she has seen in coaching are "huge." From the '50s through the '70s, practice and play were for shorter periods of time. Now there is so much required in traveling, marketing, and dealing with parents and staff that coaching gets pushed aside. The parents now are more outspoken. The coaches need more skills in conflict management to help them in business, personnel, and school negotiations.

Jaynes says she has drawn the greatest satisfaction in college basketball from teaching the players that she had in 1968–1981, working in recent years with academic women who have incredible professionalism, and seeing the accomplishments of the women she has coached and worked with.

Jaynes says that sensitivity to Title IX got her into many positions. "It has opened doors to serve on boards where I was the only female in three. I have been able to talk of Title IX's benefit for the students." There may not be any significant recent developments with regard to Title IX, says Jaynes, but compliance with Title IX requires constant vigilance from athletic directors, the NCAA women's athletic committee and the Women's Basketball Coaches Association. These groups monitor schools for compliance with Title IX. If they discover noncompliance, they try to rectify it. "You've got to constantly watch. That's the frustrating part about it. People will not just do what is right. That's truly frustrating to me."

Men's and women's basketball are not equitable right now, says Jaynes, especially in coaches' salaries. "Our survey [WBCA] says that we still make only 70 percent of what the men's coaches make no matter what our qualifications are. That's too bad. It's very bad. Unfortunately, that's also the rate that the country has right now."

Jaynes says one of the obstacles to the growth of basketball is administrators who do not believe that women should be treated equitably. While she believes that is most unfortunate, she points out that there are many, many administrations doing everything they can to really make women's sports equitable. The administrators who say, "Well, you'll have to sue me first," concern Jaynes the most. She hopes that players and the parents can change administrators' minds by bringing inequities to their attention

Like others involved in the sport, Jaynes emphasizes that Title IX has had a positive overall effect on women's basketball:

> We want to have a measuring stick. You can take our Olympic teams from 1984 to now. Title IX has made our women's sports' teams—basketball, soccer, softball—the best in the world. Those players were given an opportunity to go through college and play at the college levels. The college sport and most of the team sport arenas are our feeding grounds for the Olympic team. That's the training ground. It may not be as much as a feeder now in women's basketball because we have the WNBA, and the WNBA is probably that feeder now. Our women tend to peak in their performance when they are in their upper 20s. The WNBA is giving them that chance to perform, so therefore, our Olympic chances should escalate. But it has made us very powerful in the world in our international teams. That's the number one effect of Title IX. I cannot even begin to quote the number of athletes who have had this opportunity to compete and have had a college scholarship to go on to be coaches, teachers and doctors and nurses and ministers. We've got every profession out there where student athletes were able to get a four year degree and continue to be contributors to society because of their scholarships in women's basketball.

In addition to Title IX, says Jaynes, corporate dollars invested in basketball have contributed to its growth. "More corporations are seeing the value of women's basketball, seeing what type of sport it is. They want to be involved in it because it is American, apple pie, our graduation rates are strong, it develops incredible values as far as women are concerned. Corporations like the image we have right now with women's basketball. So we are at a stage where we are very lucky."

## DONNA A. LOPIANO[6]

"It is my hope that in the future, a woman in any society can participate in any sport without anyone discouraging her," says Dr. Donna A. Lopiano, executive director of the Women's Sports Foundation. "There would be no restrictions requiring that sports be ladylike, no concern that too much strength is required or that too much sweating would occur. Today, there are still places in the U.S. and abroad that limit the aspirations and dreams of sportswomen."

A diligent advocate of equity for women in sports, Lopiano says that the United States is ahead of most of the world because of Title IX. This law is obviously one of the primary factors that has contributed to the progress in the growth of women's college basketball. The second factor, says Lopiano, is revenue production. There were a number of colleges who promoted their women's basketball programs and demonstrated that basketball could pay for itself. Third, college women's basketball has benefitted from extensive media coverage, especially regionally televised events through the regional sport channels. This exposure has contributed to its popularity and revenue production. Another factor was the launch of two professional leagues, the ABL and the WNBA, in the wake of the well publicized performance of the Olympic gold medal U.S.A. national women's basketball teams. To all of this, add the fact that basketball enjoys the highest participation of any sport at the high school level, and you can see why women's basketball has led the explosion of interest in women's sports.

Lopiano has participated in 26 national championships in four different sports, basketball, softball, volleyball, and field hockey. In basketball, she participated in five national AAU basketball championships. In softball, Lopiano was inducted into the National Hall of Fame of the American Softball Association. She participated in ten national ASA softball championships as a member of six champion and four runner-up teams, and was a nine-time softball All-American at four different positions: pitcher, shortstop, first base and second base. She was a three-time national tournament Most Valuable Player and one-time batting champ (.429), as well as a U.S. national team player at the 1967 Pan

American Games and 1966 first world softball championships. In amateur softball, her career marks as a pitcher were 183 won and 18 lost (.910), 15–2 in national championship play, 1,633 strikeouts in 817 innings, and ERA .25 (51 earned runs in 10 years). Lopiano played professional softball for three years and participated in two national championships, both times as runner-up. In volleyball, Lopiano participated in five national USVBA championships. In field hockey, she was a participant in three national field hockey championships.

Donna A. Lopiano, executive director, Women's Sports Foundation. (Photograph: Beth Green Studios for the Women's Sports Foundation.)

In 1969-70, Lopiano was a graduate teaching assistant and the women's intramural director and women's intercollegiate volleyball coach at the University of Southern California. From 1971 to 1975, she was the assistant director of athletics and head coach of volleyball, softball, and basketball at Brooklyn College of the City University of New York. After earning her Ph.D. in physical education in 1974 from the University of Southern California, Lopiano became the Director of Intercollegiate Athletics for Women at the University of Texas at Austin. She served in that position from 1975 to 1992. While there, she hired Jody Conradt as coach of women's basketball.

Lopiano testified before Congress three times: in 1975, before the Subcommittee on Education of the Senate Committee on Labor and Public Welfare during the hearings on prohibition of sex discrimination; in 1989, before the Subcommittee on Post Secondary

Education of the Committee on Education and Labor, U.S. House, during the hearings on the roles of athletics in college life; and in 1993, before the Subcommittee, Consumer Protection and Competitiveness, U.S. House.

Lopiano has earned numerous awards and honors. She is a member of the International Scholar-Athlete Hall of Fame, Institute for International Sport, Kingston, Rhode Island (inducted June 27, 1999). *The Sporting News*, listed her among the few women in "The 100 Most Influential People in Sport," and "The 50 Most Influential People in College Sports." She received the National Association for Female Executives Award in 1995; the National Association of Collegiate Women Athletic Administrators, District 7, Administrator of the Year in 1991 and 1992; and the National Association for Girls and Women in Sport Guiding Woman in Sport Award in 1992. She was an ethics fellow at the Institute for International Sport in 1990. She was inducted into the Texas Women's Hall of Fame in 1987 by the Governor's Commission for Women. She was the recipient of the 1987 Flo Hyman Memorial Gazelle Award "to honor a person who exemplifies feminist values in athletics and scholarship," presented by the Project on Equal Education Rights of the NOW Legal Defense and Education Fund.

Lopiano currently serves as a member of 18 advisory, selection, and review boards, some of which are the committee of advisors, Positive Coaching Alliance; the National Honors Committee of the National Women's Hall of Fame; and the FIFA Women's World Cup advisory board. In the past, she served on the NCAA Gender Equity Task Force (1992 to 1993) as well as other NCAA committees and the United States Olympic Development Committee.

Lopiano has made outstanding contributions as a writer. She has published in nearly 50 different scholarly journals and sports-related media. She has produced four copyrighted videotapes on fast pitch softball.

Lopiano says that one of the greatest satisfactions of her career is being around to see the explosion of opportunity and interest in women's sports. In spite of the progress, however, Lopiano says that women's and men's basketball programs are "still highly inequitable in terms of both the funding of operating expenses and coaches' salaries. They are fairly equitable with regard to athletic scholarships." The NCAA's gender equity studies and the Women's Basketball Coaches Association salary studies substantiate her statement.

The primary obstacle that prevents women's programs from reaching equity with men's, says Lopiano, is

> the absence of leadership. There's no question that equity can happen. The question is whether athletic directors, superintendents, principals and college presidents want it to happen. Even if there was no new money available to increase opportunities for women, one could comply with Title IX by simply letting all men's and women's sports operate with smaller pieces of the financial pie. Obviously, there's a problem finding athletic directors who are willing to support budgetary cuts from men's sports. What they've done is try to get rid of some men's sports that they don't think will cause a great stir in order to maintain a high standard of living of one or two men's sports like football or basketball. To cut opportunities for men's so-called minor sports is not only anathema but contrary to the spirit of antidiscrimination law. The spirit of the law is to bring the underrepresented gender up to the level of the advantaged gender, not to make "have nots" out of those who have.

Lopiano believes the "ultimate challenge for coaches of women's basketball is to create a generation of educated athletes who understand their history, who appreciate the opportunity to play sports and the resources that are being brought to them to enable that participation. [Coaches must] be able to express to athletes how important it is for them to see themselves as role models. In their behavior and through their speaking engagements, they need to embrace a value system that they would be proud to have their own children adopt."

### BERNADETTE V. McGLADE[7]

Born in Gloucester, New Jersey, Bernadette V. McGlade describes a unique experience as a young player prior to going to high school. Her team went to a state championship basketball game. When they arrived, they discovered a problem:

> The team that I was playing for played the full court, five players, as we know the game today. It was the first year of five player basketball in New Jersey. The opposing team for the state championship game was from the northern part of the state and was still

Bernadette V. McGlade, associate commissioner, Atlantic Coast Conference.

playing half court, six players. Obviously, it was a great dilemma right on the spot. We actually played one half of the game, full court and five players and the other half six players half court. It was quite interesting. It was one of those situations where the game had to be played and the show was going to go on. That was the only way the tournament directors felt it was fair since the two teams that ended up making it through the tournament process played two different sets of rules. Something like that would certainly never happen in this day and age. In the early '70s we were so much in transition, the game was changing so quickly, that all schools did not switch to the five player game at the same time. I suppose that could be considered an historical game!

An NWIT All-American in 1980 at the University of North Carolina at Chapel Hill, she still holds the school's career record—women's and men's—for rebounds with 1,251. McGlade earned both her undergraduate and graduate degrees at North Carolina, where her playing jersey hangs from the rafters. She says the game has "changed light years" just in the short time from when she played basketball (1976–1980) until now. She says, "The nature of the game, the competitive spirit hasn't changed. Every player thinks she has the chance to win and be successful, and relatively speaking, the competitiveness is the same. However, the support and the advances that have come into the game as a result of Title IX are unprecedented."

The types of changes that are precedent setting, says McGlade, are the funding for the programs including scholarships; the way

teams travel, from traveling on buses to traveling on private char-
tered planes; the type of equipment that's available; and the types
of support services. Explaining the changes in support services,
McGlade says that when she was a player, everyone on the team,
for the most part, trained herself in terms of conditioning and
weight training: "You sort of read books and trained any way you
knew how to do it best. These days there are full time weight,
strength and conditioning coaches on staff as well as the full time
head basketball coaches and assistants."

Yet, McGlade says that she was "one of the lucky ones. I was
entering college and as a result of Title IX, I was able to earn a
scholarship and went to UNC. So, certainly, Title IX and playing
basketball were responsible for financially covering the major cost
of my education."

From 1981 to 1988, McGlade served as Georgia Tech's first
full-time women's basketball coach. Only 22 when hired, she was
the youngest Division I head coach. In 1985, she was promoted to
assistant director in charge of Tech's Olympic sports programs,
and in 1987, she took responsibilities for all sports programs operations, NCAA compliance and the Total Person program as associate director. McGlade served on many ACC/NCAA committees:
Women's Basketball, Television, Gender Equity, NCAA Compliance and the Committee on Women's Athletics. She has been
inducted into the South Jersey Women's Basketball Hall of Fame
and the Georgia Tech Hall of Fame. In 1987, she was honored as
an Image Maker for the city of Atlanta.

Having the opportunity to make a difference in young women's
lives has given McGlade the most satisfaction in her coaching
career:

> Not only student athletes that played for me or that I recruited, but
> also being able to impact and see the difference with parents, fans
> and supporters of the game. There aren't many professions where
> you get to really have a direct influence—sometimes on the course
> of a young person's attitude and the direction she is going to take.
> So that, without a doubt, is my greatest satisfaction from coaching,
> and it still is to this day. Our athletes are future leaders, they
> are future good citizens, and so many lessons are learned through
> sports. It's really, truly, like a family, and that's not a cliché;
> you live and breathe [your team] every second, seven days a week,
> 24 hours a day when you're in charge of a team as the coach. It's

very much like being a parent. The pressure and responsibility level is very high.

In 1997, the Atlantic Coast Conference appointed McGlade its first-ever associate commissioner for women's basketball operations. At the time she was serving as Georgia Tech's senior associate director of athletics. Today, McGlade chairs the NCAA Division I Women's Basketball Committee, is a member of the NCAA Basketball Issues Group and the NCAA Basketball Marketing Committee and the NCAA Television Negotiations Committee.

In 1993, McGlade was tournament director for the NCAA Division I Women's Basketball Final Four in Atlanta, which obtained the first pre-game sellout in the history of the event. Of the sellout she says, "Ever since then, the Final Four has been sold out; it sort of took off at that time. It was a strategic process that we went through to host the event. The women's Final Four had gone through a series of years where it was still an event that needed a lot of work in terms of putting capacity crowds in the arena. The sell-out and success of the 1993 Final Four was a great accomplishment for the city of Atlanta and for Georgia Tech."

That same year, McGlade was recognized for the Excellence in Education Award for the development of an Atlanta Public School Outreach program. Later, she served for a year and a half as the 1996 Olympic Games liaison for the Georgia Tech Athletic Association, coordinating the department strategic plan.

McGlade offers an inspiring summary of her philosophy:

> Never underestimate the will of the human spirit. If we know ahead of time who's going to win and lose, there's really not a point to lacing up your shoes and playing the game. We see time and time again that you can calculate all you want statistically, you can calculate all you want on paper and strategize all you want with the players that a coach would have for a game, but you just can't underestimate an individual's will, her spirit and her tenacity to want to achieve something great.

### SUE RODIN[8]

"I am a pre–Title IX baby," says Sue Rodin, president of Stars and Strategies, Inc., and the founder and president of Women in

Sports and Events (WISE). "As a result of not being a direct beneficiary of Title IX, I focus my business on women's sports, and on helping young athletes who *have* benefitted [from Title IX] to enhance their marketing appeal. So, indirectly—maybe it's vicarious on my part—and in subjective, subtle ways, Title IX has definitely affected my business." Rodin founded WISE, a national networking organization for female executives, in 1993. The professional organization connects women in the business of sports and special events.

Sue Rodin, founder and president, WISE (Women in Sports Events), and president, Stars and Strategies, Sports Marketing and Management.

Among the elite athletes for whom Rodin is the exclusive marketing representative are four members of the World Cup soccer championship team, including Julie Foudy and Carla Overbeck. She also represents superstar swimmer Jenny Thompson (5 Olympic gold medals), as well as WNBA player and NCAA champion basketball standout Stephanie White-McCarty.

Each year WISE presents its Woman of the Year Award. In 1998, WISE recognized the achievements of three women, including Val Ackerman, president of the Women's National Basketball Association.

A graduate of Ohio State University, Rodin earned a master's degree from the University of Massachusetts at Amherst. "When I played basketball, it was the half court game, a limited number of dribbles—a very, very different creature than what we have today," she says. Rodin says that Title IX has had a tremendous impact on women's college basketball programs. There are more opportunities and more scholarships over the past quarter century and with that comes more television exposure which greatly enhances the visibility and the acceptance of the sport. Without a doubt, says Rodin, Title IX has been a tremendous boost to women's basketball as well as to other sports.

Among the factors other than Title IX that have contributed to the progress in the growth of women's college basketball, says Rodin, is television. "Television is very, very critical to the success of any sport. For better or worse, Americans define what's important by coverage, and if you're not on TV, it's almost as if you do not exist, because there are just so many people that can attend an event. The fact that ESPN has covered more and more of the basketball games has been a tremendous boost."

Although basketball is just a fraction of what Rodin's business is all about, she hopes that "the growth of women's basketball continues to reach wider audiences and that it reaches a level equal to what the men have done thus far."

# Men of the Game

### Geno Auriemma[9]

Geno Auriemma, the head coach of women's basketball at the University of Connecticut, marked his 15th season as Husky head coach in 1999. A two-time National Coach of the Year, he was named Naismith National Coach of the Year and Associated Press National Coach of the Year in 1994-95 and 1996-97. He was also the Women's Basketball Coaches Association National Coach of the Year in 1996-97 and 1999-2000, and received the Victor Award in 1994-95 and 1995-96.

Auriemma's 14 year record of 357–94 (.792) places him at No. 3 in winning percentage among active Division I coaches. In 1995, his team won the NCAA national championship with a 35–0 record. His teams have made three NCAA Final Four appearances and six NCAA Elite Eight appearances. Perhaps one of his most significant achievements, among his many honors and record-setting games, is the fact that his teams have a 100 percent graduation rate for all the recruited student-athletes who completed their eligibility at Connecticut. Since 1991-92, 20 of the 30 starting players (10 different players) have been on the Dean's List. The fan support for his team, as measured by home attendance, is No. 2 nationally for all Division I games.

On January 10, 1999, *The New York Post* said, "Geno Auriemma says his idea of 'fun' is to come into practice every day and put his players in 'impossible situations' so they fail over and over again. 'I'll keep doing it until my players start saying, 'Hey, this is cool. I'm going to figure a way out of this.' 'I want to find their breaking point and extend it in practice, so that in games, frustrating situations seem easy.'"

In 1998, Auriemma arranged for injured Nykesha Sales, the all–American forward, to score off the game open-

Geno Auriemma, head coach, women's basketball, University of Connecticut.

ing. Sales had ruptured an Achilles tendon, possibly ending her career at UConn. She was one point short of the school scoring record. Auriemma said, "I don't care about the criticism. You've got to do the right thing for the kids. She never asked to score a lot of points and she never asked to break the record. It was the right thing to do for all she has done for UConn the last four years."

Auriemma graduated from West Chester College, Pennsylvania, with a B.A. in political science. From 1981 to 1985, he served as the primary assistant women's coach at the University of Virginia under Debbie Ryan. He came to Virginia from St. Joseph's University in Philadelphia, where he was an assistant coach of women's basketball with head coach Jim Foster, who now coaches women's basketball at Vanderbilt. From 1979 to 1981, he coached boys' basketball at Bishop Kenrick High School in Norristown, Pennsylvania, his alma mater.

In April of 1996, Auriemma was co–head coach of the National Senior All-Stars (with Tennessee's Pat Summitt) when the All-Stars met the United States National Team. During the summer of 1996, he served as coach of the USA Basketball Select Team in Colorado Springs, Colorado. In January of 1995, Auriemma was named an assistant coach of the USA World University Games Women's Basketball Team, which played in Fukuoka, Japan, in the summer of 1995, but circumstances caused him to relinquish that position. He also served as head coach of the West Team at the U.S. Olympic Festival in San Antonio, Texas.

### LEON BARMORE[10]

Leon Barmore, the head coach for women's basketball at Louisiana Tech University, believes that the way to win is to prepare

**Leon Barmore, head coach, women's basketball, Louisiana Tech University. (Phototgraph: Juan Ocampo.)**

the team to win. He cherishes his accomplishments. His records mean a lot to him. He says that coaching is a "rewarding business. It is difficult, but there are many rewards. You must have heart and really care for your players. You have to push them. Being a coach that gets on his players doesn't mean you don't love them. It is a way to get the most out of them."

Barmore has led the Techsters to 11 30-plus win seasons, nine Final Fours, and a national championship in 1988 with a 17 year coaching record of 489–74 (.869). He is the winningest coach in the history of men's or women's basketball. He was the quickest coach to reach 450 victories, doing so in his 520th game. He holds a record of .750 in NCAA tournament games. In eight seasons, his teams have won five tournament Sun Belt Conference crowns and seven straight regular season titles.

A credit to Barmore's success is his hiring of top caliber assistant coaches who he says are "invaluable" to the program. In 1999, Kim Mulkey-Robertson marked her 15th season. Two first-time assistant coaches that year were Chris Long and Jessie Kenlaw.

Barmore is a six-time Sun Belt Conference Coach of the Year. He was named Co-Coach of the Decade for the 1980s by the U.S. Basketball Writers Association. The USBWA has also awarded him three national Coach of the Year titles (1988, 1990, and 1996). In 1988, he was named Naismith National Coach of the Year.

As a player at Ruston High School in Ruston, Louisiana, he earned all-state honors while leading his team to a pair of state championships. As a college player at Louisiana Tech, he was captain and led the team to all–Gulf States Conference honors.

After graduation, he coached the boys' team at Bastrop High School, Louisiana from 1967 to 1971, to a 84–41 record. From 1971 to 1977 he coached at Ruston High, his alma mater, and led his team to a 148–49 record. He first coached the women's team at Tech University as an assistant in 1977. He became an associate head coach in 1980, and a co–head coach in 1982.

Barmore says the game has changed today from when he started coaching. "There are more teams and more athletes—better athletes." The game is faster and more athletic. He believes the best is yet to come, "It isn't even close to reaching its peak. The quality of play is just going to get better and better. I'm convinced that within the next 5 to 10 years, you'll go to a game and instead of seeing maybe one Sheryl Swoopes out there, you'll see several."

He believes in hard work for his team and says, "Once they learn the work ethic that we need here, then we will have a very good basketball team." Game day should not be a letdown "when you prepare as much as we do."

Barmore has won without a big budget, luxurious facilities, or a lot of media coverage. Tech is a small school in a small town that has won anyway.

In 1999, Barmore said that basketball is really about the players. He says, "We had a banquet this year where about 80 percent of our former players came back and they talked about the program and its history. That was when I saw a change in our players this year, realizing their heritage and what it takes to keep it going."

## TONY DICECCO[11]

"People ask me a lot, 'Do you have any children?' And I say, 'Well, I have 15, and a majority of them come in around August and they usually leave me around the middle of May.'" As head coach of the women's basketball team at the University of Northern Iowa, Tony DiCecco, or "Tony D." as he is called, says he tries to bring out a team atmosphere that is based on a family atmosphere. "If we can give a little bit of those values, kids can understand that you have those good times and you have those bad times, but you learn to do things together. The strength that you have in that unit a lot of times can get you through any problems you may come across."

Tony D.'s tremendous love and passion for the game led him to coach women's basketball. "I love to teach. I very rarely refer to myself as a coach. I am a teacher. I'm a teacher of the game," he says. He was an elementary, junior high, and high school teacher for 18 years before getting into the college game as an assistant coach at Creighton University in Omaha, Nebraska. For six years there, he developed a great love for the college game. Tony D. says that student athletes are "a lot more focused on what they want to accomplish. A lot are equally focused on what their degree is going to give them as well as what basketball is going to give them. That's exciting."

A 1971 graduate of Upper Iowa University in Fayette, Iowa, DiCecco served from 1971 to 1973 as head girls' softball coach at West Central High in Maynard, Iowa, where his 1973 team finished third in the Iowa State Softball Tournament. As a head girls' basketball coach from 1974 to 1989 at Montezuma High School, Iowa, he compiled a 306–69 record (including eight conference, 10 sectional and two regional championships), and made two Iowa State Tournament appearances.

During Tony D.'s tenure at Creighton University as an assistant coach, the Lady Jays compiled a 122–52 record, including two regular season Western Athletic Conference (WAC) championships, one WAC Tournament Championship and two NCAA tournament appearances. Nine players were named first-team All-Missouri Valley Conference or All-Western Athletic Conference. During this period, Tony D. developed a four-year program to elevate awareness of the women's basketball program in the Omaha area. Through his efforts, attendance at women's basketball games doubled during the first year of his promotions.

Tony DiCecco, head women's basketball coach, University of Northern Iowa.

Tony D. became head coach of women's basketball at the University of Northern Iowa in 1995. At Northern Iowa, he has had 15 players named to the Missouri Valley Conference Academic All-Conference teams. The women's basketball program went from 4–22 the season before his arrival to a 19–8 mark in the 1998-1999 season. He improved the Panther victory total by at least three each season and led the team to consecutive winning seasons in 1998 and 1999 for the first time since 1982 and 1983. DiCecco tied for the third-winningest coach in UNI's history with a 78–76 (.506) record in four years. Attendance records have been broken. In

1998-1999, the team drew over 15,000 in total attendance and had the first-ever home sellout with 2,225 fans against Iowa State.

DiCecco's improvements were recognized by his university's selection to the 1999 Women's Preseason National Invitation Tournament. His 1999-2000 team participated in tournaments hosted by the University of Missouri-Kansas City (UMKC) and Syracuse. In past years, his teams have appeared in non-conference tournaments in Kansas, Nevada and Florida. He credits his success to the team, his assistant coaches, Colleen Heimstead and Tanya Warren, and his graduate assistant coach Kelley Wethoff, all members of the family atmosphere.

DiCecco believes that the most important thing coaches can teach student athletes is that when they have excitement, passion and love for what they do, they have a greater chance at being successful—whether it's basketball, academics or the workplace. "All young women have the ability to dream and see themselves as being the best at what they do. I'm one of the biggest dreamers there is. I love to dream and I love to think about the possibility that someday the University of Northern Iowa might be in the NCAA tournament." DiCecco says that it has been very exciting to change Northern Iowa's team into winners:

> When I first came, we dreamed about winning ten games, and we dreamed about some year winning 20. We haven't won 20 yet, but we won 19 last year. Over the previous 15 years when UNI was in a 10 team league, we were either ninth or tenth. Would we ever get off that bottom? Last year we were third, the highest ever in the history of the school. Those are the things that I dream about.
>
> I dream about going to the NCAA. When I was at Creighton, I had a chance to go to the NCAA. And I'm telling you, *Wow*—there's just no other word. I mean, being a part of the highest level of competition and being a part of the NCAA was a great experience for me. I want to do whatever I can to have the University of Northern Iowa experience that. We've now been selected in the first-ever pre- or post-season tournament in school history. We're now one of 16 teams that have been invited this year to participate in the pre-season NIT [National Invitation Tournament]. I dreamt about that.
>
> Student athletes have to understand what a great feeling it is to dream about something, and dream about being the best. There's an excitement about people that do that. I like sharing this excitement with other people. And I'd like the student athletes in our program to experience it.

# Conclusion

These profiles of athletic administrators and other professionals reveal the intricate interrelationship of administration and the game of basketball. The women profiled in this chapter have all participated in sports, and most played and coached basketball. Their love of the game is apparent in their continued efforts to see it through many growing pains and in their ongoing joy for its successes.

Men continue to coach in the women's game. Successful teachers, they contribute to the growth of the women's game. Their profiles give a glimpse of their dedication to the players and to the game.

In Chapter 5, women coaches of women's teams and one woman coach of a men's team are profiled.

# Chapter 5

# *Women Coaches: Selected Profiles*

*"Winners are not born, they are self-made."*
Pat Summitt, Head Coach
Women's Basketball
University of Tennessee[1]

The early years of the twenty-first century promise to be good ones for women's basketball. Both experienced and novice coaches find themselves teaching a world popular sport at a time when society cheers the female athlete. True to its history, however, the sport continues to change.

The phenomenal growth of women's basketball can be attributed to the coaches who molded their players into outstanding teams that captured the attention of their universities and the nation. There are many such coaches in college women's basketball, far more than this book can hope to cover. Many coaches across the country in all ranks on numerous college campuses teach young athletes not only the values of playing the game season after season, but also how those values can be applied to life after the game.

Primarily women are coaches of women's teams, although this

chapter will examine one coach belonging to the minority of women that coach men's teams. The profiles are selected, but there are many other women that could be included. Not only are there numerous good coaches in women's basketball, but there are many ways to evaluate what makes a good coach. As Tony DiCecco, University of Northern Iowa head basketball coach for women, says, "There are so many ways to look at the coach. Do you look at the X and O coach, do you look at the motivator, do you look at the teacher? I think the great ones have the ability to steal a little bit from each one of those categories."[2] You can look at the record of the team, says DiCecco, but you have to consider the quality of the player. DiCecco describes the teams that go to the Final Four: "They do some of the same drills that we do. They do the exact same things in practice. It's who they're doing those drills with that makes a tremendous difference. The level of player is the difference." Good players are a direct result of good recruiting, which has a direct relationship to the amount of available funds to attract good players (and good coaches). It is not my intention to neglect the contribution of assistant coaches. As Pat Summitt says in her book *Raise the Roof*, "Assistant coaches have the most thankless job in the business. They work long hours and make crucial contributions under pressure, they do it for considerably less pay than the head coach, and they get absolutely no credit."[3] Thus, I ask you to keep in mind those assistants, as well as the countless great college women basketball coaches in the nation who may be great technicians, great motivators, great teachers, but lack the resources to attract quality players, or else simply lack experience. As Gail Goestenkors of Duke University says, "There are a lot of young coaches out there that just haven't made a name for themselves, that just haven't had that longevity."[4]

The coaches I have chosen for this book have been selected for a range of reasons. They are a fairly diverse group. Some are young; some have been coaches for decades. Most are active, but some are retired. At least one coaches a men's team.

# Women Coaches of Men's Teams

Acosta and Carpenter found in 1998 that the percentage of women coaching men's teams within the NCAA stood at 2 percent. All were head coaches, and almost all were coaching combined

Kerri-Ann McTiernan, head coach, men's basketball, Kingsborough Community College, The City University of New York.

teams (men's and women's teams that practice together such as swimming, track, tennis, and cross country).[5] In 1996, *The Chronicle for Higher Education* reported that Kingsborough Community College of the City of New York (CUNY) had hired Kerri McTiernan as head coach of their men's basketball team and that "McTiernan is the first woman all throughout the United States to hold the position."[6] McTiernan had coached women's basketball until funds cut their program.[7] According to the *Chronicle*, two other women coached men's basketball teams: Bernadette Locke-Mattox, assistant to Rick Pitino at the University of Kentucky, and Leslie Crandell, assistant coach at Westmont College.

*Sports Illustrated* reported in 1996 that University of Tennessee athletic director Doug Dickey had approached Pat Summitt to coach the Volunteer men, but she declined.[8] Summitt acknowledged that society thinks coaching a men's team is a step up because the men's game is more popular, but for her this was insufficient reason to give up a valuable job that she loves.[9]

When *Sports Illustrated* asked male athletic directors why so few women are coaching men's teams, some claimed that no women applied for the jobs. Others cited a preference for men coaches to coach men's teams and women coaches to coach women's teams. Some said simply that they had never thought about it. But as *Sports Illustrated* points out, coaches such as Connecticut's Geno Auriemma and Louisiana Tech's Leon Barmore have overcome gender difference with players, "so why couldn't women coaches succeed similarly with male players?" The reasons offered by athletic directors—a woman can't motivate men, can't recruit men, and can't teach a fast game that's played above the rim—sell both female coaches and male players short.

Kingsborough Community College of CUNY is a two year school, where student athletes earn associates degrees. It is a member of the National Junior College Athletic Association (NCJAA), an organization first conceived in 1937 at Fresno, California, as an association that would promote and supervise a national program of junior college sports and activities consistent with the educational objectives of junior colleges."[10] Coach Kerri-Ann McTiernan sees her role in the junior college as vital: "They can do two years of their eligibility playing here. The focus that I try to concentrate on for my team is, of course, to win at this level and to make regional playoffs, but also to get my guys to get their associate's degree, and get them ready for a four year education, to move on to a four year school to hopefully play ball at a higher level, and then also to receive a four year degree and improve their education."[11]

McTiernan acknowledges that coaching a men's team is different in some ways from coaching women, particularly in areas of speed and strength. Nevertheless, her views on coaching are not unlike those of women coaching women's teams. Male or female, says McTiernan, it takes the same qualities to make a good coach:

> I think you have to love what you do, because people read into that. You've got to be honest with who you are, honest with the expectations; lay them out for your players, the student athletes, and yourself. Besides having knowledge of the game, you have to be able to communicate. The important thing is we do it because we love the game and we love the kids. I think that most coaches you come across feel like they have a very satisfying job because they feel like they make a difference. You make the student athletes better basketball players, but it is so much more than that. And the reason we can give back is that sports has given us as much. Sports should help us grow just as much as the kids. One thing that I think is important to recognize is that good coaches are good coaches because of the same qualities; it's all the same.[12]

# Women Coaches of Women's Teams

## CEAL BARRY[13]

"Love of the challenge" describes Ceal Barry's coaching style and her life style. Being satisfied with where you are, that is, where the sport is, capsulizes another part of her philosophy. Remaining in coaching at one university, says Barry, is a challenge:

> If you reminisce about all of the games won, championships won, or the NCAA tournament games won, those wins are part of coaching. The relationships developed are important to me. Someday when I look back, I think I'm going to be most proud of the longevity. Particularly, I hoped to choose a university, as I did in 1983, work through any potential hurdles and demonstrate commitment and loyalty. It might be easier to say, "I don't like these facilities; our budget's not high enough," and then jump at the next opportunity. I wanted to avoid that type of attitude. To me, that's my greatest achievement.

Ceal Barry, head coach, women's basketball, University of Colorado.

Barry came to the University of Colorado in 1983. Her beginning could have been one of many rungs in the ladder of a successful career, but, because of Barry's love of the challenge and loyalty to building Colorado's program, she has stayed at Colorado. *The Denver Post* named her the most powerful woman in Colorado sports. She has developed a program that half a million fans have come to see. To a reporter from *The Denver Post*, Barry commented, "There's some principle about sticking to the job I committed to when I was 28 years old."

Born in Louisville, Kentucky, Barry played guard and graduated from Assumption High School in 1973. She received her B.S. degree in accounting in 1977. Barry says of her college years, "I started on the team at the University of Kentucky for four years. I was a guard for four years and captain of my team in my junior and senior year. I was one of the first females to receive a scholarship at Kentucky in my senior year, when I received tuition and fees and was awarded a $750 scholarship. That was an achievement, to be one of the first women [to receive a scholarship] particularly in a state like Kentucky and a university like Kentucky that prides itself on basketball."

Barry received her M. Ed. degree in 1979 from the University of Cincinnati, where from 1977 to 1979 she was the graduate assistant coach. From 1979 to 1983 she served as head coach at the University of Cincinnati. She was the Bearcats' winningest coach with an 83–42 record in four seasons. Her 16 season record at Colorado, 316–169 (.652), is notable. Her total career record through the 1998-1999 season is an impressive 399–211 (.652). The Buffaloes have had nine 20-win seasons, a school record 30 wins in 1995, four Big Eight regular season titles including the 1993, 1994 and 1995 three-peat and five conference tournament titles (1989, 1992, 1995, 1996, 1997), including the inaugural Big 12 tournament trophy in 1997. A four-time Big Eight Coach of the Year (1989, 1993, 1994, 1995), Barry was also named the Converse District V Coach of the Year in 1993 and 1995. Her 13 season Big Eight record is spectacular. She coached the only two teams to go undefeated in league play (14–0) in 1989 and 1995; she won more regular season games (118), league titles (4), tournament titles (4), and Coach-of-the-Year honors (4), and coached more Newcomers of the Year (4), than any league coach during the same span and was tied for most Big Eight tournament MVPs (4), NCAA tournament appearances (7) and first team Kodak All-Americans (1).

When the Big Eight became the Big 12, Barry's accomplishments followed when Colorado was the only conference team to advance to the 1997 NCAA Sweet 16. Her eight NCAA championship tournaments include four appearances in the Sweet 16 (1993, 1994, 1995 and 1997) and two trips to the Elite Eight (1993, 1995). She has three wins over past defending national champions, most recently Stanford, 80–67, in the program's first regional appearance at the 1993 NCAA West Regional semifinal in Missoula, Montana.

The Women's Basketball Coaches Association in 1994 awarded Barry the Carol Eckman Award. She was assistant coach for the 1996 gold medal winning United States Olympic Women's Basketball Team, her seventh USA Basketball coaching appointment since 1987. She assisted Tara VanDerveer of Stanford in the games of the twenty-sixth Olympiad in Atlanta.

It was at this pivotal point that Barry's philosophy of commitment to the student athlete and to Colorado surfaced again as she withdrew from consideration to become the head coach of the USA Basketball women's program. The position would have committed the next four years of her career. She has also declined repeated attempts by the ABL and WNBA to persuade her to coach professional basketball. Her own words as to what has been and continues to be important are, "I'm committed to the philosophy of basketball being an educational opportunity in a player's life. That would be descriptive of my contribution to the game. Secondly, I've contributed to the growth of the game in the Rocky Mountain region, in particular, in the state of Colorado."

What brings Barry the greatest satisfaction? Again the word "challenge" surfaces:

> Being able to face the day to day challenge of running a major Division I basketball program. To take a team and really strive to overachieve. That's really my goal every year. To be able to live in Boulder and take the players that we recruit and try to overachieve on a national level. To me, that's the satisfaction that I get. I've chosen to live here because it's a great place to live. Yet, I still feel I can take a team and get them at the top level of basketball. That's a satisfaction to me. My greatest challenge and my greatest satisfaction have been being able to have teams in the '90s that have competed on the national level, competed in the NCAA tournament, really make a run in the Final Four, and do those things. I've enjoyed that challenge.

Barry also takes satisfaction from her long-term success in the profession:

> A personal achievement is being able to stay employed in a profession that is constantly under scrutiny. There are not very many coaches, particularly women, that have been able or have had the opportunity to be employed that long. I'm proud of the fact that I

could coach from the '70s prior to the inclusion of women's basketball in the NCAA. Going from AIAW to NCAA in the '80s, to the growth of the game in the '90s with the increased media, and then into the next century, probably.

Barry's final comments clearly demonstrate her commitment to college basketball, and why she so values the game:

> I hope the values are that we continue to keep women in the game and that coaches don't lose sight of the intent and the purpose and the values of sport in teaching young people, because it has such an impact on society. Athletics has such a tremendous impact on the American society that I think the future of our society can benefit from outstanding athletes going on and being leaders in their communities. The biggest influence and impact on those athletes is the head coach. I hope coaches never lose sight of their responsibility to that end. It's not money, it's not power, it's not influence. Those things are so small in comparison to what the real contribution to our society should be.

## LYNN BRIA[14]

To become head coach of women's basketball at Ohio University, Lynn Bria rose from humble beginnings that equipped her with a sense of teamwork. She explains:

> The fact that I'm even really here in Division I basketball is amazing because I came from a really small town in West Virginia. To come from there to here, I'm very proud of that. It's the one thing I'm most proud of. This business is very competitive and it's very hard to get into and the longer I'm in, the more knowledge I have of that and am aware of that. I look back and see that I've had a lot of help from people. I certainly don't think anyone can do this on her own.

Bria was one of nine children born to Sam and Jo Nancy Bria. At the time she was hired at Ohio University, Bria said, "It's great to be closer to home." A 1985 Charleston Catholic High School graduate and a 1990 graduate of the University of Charleston (West Virginia), Bria was named to the first team of the All-West Virginia Intercollegiate Athletics Conference as a senior and twice named to the honorable mention team. She helped the Golden

Lynn Bria, head coach, women's basketball, Ohio University.

Eagles to the NAIA national tournament two times and was named to the conference all-tournament team as a junior. Bria was also a tennis player. She was named all-conference in that sport as a senior and helped her team get to the national tournament.

Bria was an assistant coach for one year at Radford University (Virginia) and for two seasons at Marshall University (West Virginia). Bria spent three seasons as head coach at Texas Women's University in Denton, Texas, before going to the University of Central Florida in Orlando in 1996 for three seasons.

Bria's coaching led the University of Central Florida to the 1999 NCAA Tournament. Bria was the second-winningest women's basketball coach in school history. Her 50–36 record in three seasons led the Golden Knights to post-season play in 1998-1999 by winning the Trans America Athletic Conference regular season and post-season tournament titles and advancing to the NCAA tournament's field of 64. UCF lost to Louisiana Tech in the Final Four, but finished with a 20–10 overall record and a 13–3 TAAC regular season record. It was the first team in school history to win the TAAC championship and the second to reach the NCAA tournament. Bria's three-year regular season record in TAAC play was 33–15 (.687).

"Lynn Bria is an up and coming star in women's basketball," Orlando Magic general manager Pat Williams said of Bria when Ohio University chose her in 1999 as their eighth women's basketball coach. "She's a tremendous person and will do a wonderful job. She has an unlimited future and will go to any heights in the game that she wants to and it is a wonderful hire for Ohio University."

Bria loves the game, but like most varsity coaches, she cares most about the student athletes and their future:

> I'm really in this for the people and for the players. I always say my favorite people in the world next to my immediate family are players and coaches. They mean more to me than anything. Sometimes it's years down the road when players call you and just say thanks or they understand why we did that or that they still do that. You give them a form of guidance and some guidelines and help direct them or just help them, because they bring a lot of problems of their own. That is the most significant contribution I can make and probably it gives me the greatest satisfaction. When you see them improve on the basketball court, that's satisfying, but not like when you see them improve as people, or when you see them choose a better way. That's really the most gratifying thing.

## JODY CONRADT[15]

"There have been some championships and some significant games, but those are all sort of pale in comparison to the big picture. In my mind, my most outstanding achievement has been being able to be a small part of changing the perception of women's sports, building a fan base, and providing opportunities for young women to showcase their talent, to get scholarships and to become themselves, role models," says Jody Conradt, head coach and director of women's athletics at the University of Texas. She says she feels fortunate to be at a university that was willing to provide the resources and opportunity for us to build a program. The program's visibility has allowed it to be a model for other programs. "We started to show that people would care about reporting and attending women's events. I think we were able to attract the kind of athletes who started to show the world that women can be extremely talented and involved in team sports in ways that our society can relate to."

When she came to the University of Texas in 1976, Conradt says, there was little visibility for or awareness of women's sports, and opportunities for women to participate in sport were limited. "That's changed dramatically. It's almost like being a part of history."

Conradt grew up in Goldthwaite, Texas, and credits her

Jody Conradt, head coach, women's basketball, the University of
Texas–Austin.

mother, Ann Conradt, who played on a city softball team, for her competitiveness. Conradt saw her mother as an athlete and assumed that her mother's diligence and intensity happened everywhere. "When she got on task, nothing deterred her from that," she said. "She might not have always been competing in sports, might not have been competing against someone else, but she competed with herself and challenged herself." Conradt played ball in the yard with her father, Charles Conradt, who played on a semi-pro baseball team.

Conradt also played basketball in the yard and dreamed of becoming a player. She first had an inkling of how far her dreams could go when Marie Reynolds, a native of Goldthwaite, returned after touring with a women's basketball team, the All-American Redheads. Most women who grew up in Goldthwaite remained there, said Conradt. "But here was this woman and it was like she had made the big time. She wasn't a redhead, but she was a good basketball player."

Conradt was a 40-point-per-game scorer at Goldthwaite High School. At Baylor, she signed up for an intramural team, but instead was signed up for the "extra-mural" team which today is called the varsity squad. She averaged 20 points per game. She was planning to major in history because most women she knew with college degrees became teachers. "Some professions were not women's careers when I was growing up. I didn't see women doctors, women pilots, or women lawyers. All of those professions are fairly commonplace now," Conradt said. "Women with careers in sports also inspired other women to believe that they could do things that were nontraditional."

Conradt played on a divided court with six players playing on half of the court. "There was a perception that women could not be strong enough or well conditioned enough to run the whole court, which is pretty humorous now and makes us all chuckle to think about—to think that we bought into that," she says.

"Changes in coaching have not been dramatic," says Conradt.

> The game is a game that has a history, and that history has dictated that it be played on a court that didn't ever change size, and the goal has not changed in height. The most significant change is players have become more talented. They are able to perform more difficult skills with greater consistency and efficiency. But as far as

the strategies of the game, there haven't been dramatic changes, not even to the extent that there have been changes in the men's game. When the men became stronger and bigger, they started to dunk. The women haven't been able to do that on any consistent basis, so, therefore, we're still talking about performing basic basketball skills in a way that allows you to play the game. We change defenses. We have different defensive philosophies. We see universal offenses. Coaches all tend to copy each other and learn from each other, so it's not as though there have been dramatic changes in the game itself. The dramatic change has been how the players play the game.

Conradt graduated from Baylor with a degree in physical education in 1963. She first taught and coached at Waco Midway High School before returning to Baylor to receive her master's degree in 1969. At Sam Houston State in Huntsville, Texas, she had her first head coaching position from 1969 to 1972. Her win-loss record for those four years was a 74–23. She taught seven classes and coached volleyball, track and basketball. Players took their own cars to away games, and there was no athletic budget for women's sports.

Conradt's record at the University of Texas at Arlington from 1973 to 1976 was 43–39. In 1976, Texas women's athletic director Donna Lopiano (now head of the Women's Sports Foundation) hired Conradt. Lopiano and Conradt built Texas women's basketball into a major program. Successful promotional efforts produced crowds that averaged more than 8,000 per game, and Conradt's teams played innovative, full-court pressing, fast breaking basketball. Conradt used tactics almost no one in the women's game in the late 1970s and early 1980s was stressing, such as the double low post, a transition game and a full court pressing defense.

Conradt has more wins, 725, than any women's coach in history. She has had 20 seasons of 20 wins or more at Texas with her University of Texas record at 608–160 (.792) entering the 1999-2000 season. Overall, Conradt's record stood at 725–222 (.766) entering the 1999-2000 year. She is the all-time winningest coach in women's college basketball in NCAA Division I history. In 1986, she coached Texas to the NCAA title with a perfect 34–0 record. She has averaged 27 victories a year at Texas and has taken her team to 15 of 17 NCAA tournaments from 1982 to 1999.

In 1980, 1984 and 1986, she was National Coach of the Year. In 1986 and 1987 she made two Final Four appearances. In 1995, she was inducted into the International Women's Sports Hall of Fame. In 1997, she was inducted into the Texas Sports Hall of Fame. In 1998, Conradt was inducted into the Naismith Basketball Hall of Fame, making her one of only three women's coaches in the prestigious Hall. (One of the other coaches, inducted in 1984, was the late Margaret Wade, who coached Delta State in Mississippi to three national championships in the 1970s.) In June of 1999, Conradt was inducted into the Women's Basketball Hall of Fame in its inaugural year of nominations.

Conradt says that although Title IX "absolutely" had an impact on her career,

> it probably didn't have any effect on the fact that I stayed involved in sport or chose sport. It was my passion. We do the things we are passionate about, and it is wonderful to make a living doing the things we are passionate about. I grew up playing. I wanted to stay involved. I don't think we can ever get so wrapped up in what we do to think that we're there; we are just on the way. And the journey has to continue. It has to continue from this generation to the next. We have made tremendous progress; but women's basketball is a work in progress, it is not a job completed. Women should pursue their passion, and accept no boundaries.

### GAIL GOESTENKORS[16]

Gail Goestenkors, head coach of women's basketball at Duke University, says that her love of basketball began at an early age in Waterford, Michigan. Her first opportunity to play it as an organized sport, however, came "in the middle of reform":

> When Title IX came out in 1972, I was nine years old. I ran track in seventh grade. There was no girls' track team, so I had to run on the boys' team. In eighth grade, the school was forced to implement girls' track, and I know that was a result of Title IX. Then they had no girls' basketball team and they wouldn't let me play on the boys' team. It wasn't until my ninth grade year that they began a girls' basketball team. It was a process. I was kind of right in the middle of all of it. I was usually playing with and against boys when they would let me play. Now, fortunately, little girls get to play organized basketball as young as the boys do.

Goestenkors attended high school at Kettering, Michigan. She played point guard in college under former Purdue head coach

**Gail Goestenkors, head women's basketball coach, Duke University.**

Marsha Reall for four seasons at Saginaw Valley State, Michigan, from 1981 to 1985. She earned NAIA All-American honors, was team and conference MVP, and was an Academic All-Conference selection. She led her teams to a record of 114–13 with a second place, a third place and two quarterfinal finishes at the NAIA National Championships. Goestenkors says of her days as a college player:

We had no fans in the stands. As a matter of fact, when I first started, I walked on. I didn't have a scholarship. Scholarships were just becoming available at that time in college for women basketball players. So, my first year, I was a walk on, and received a scholarship my second year and from then on was on scholarship. We played purely for the love of the game. It wasn't about necessarily getting the scholarship or playing for the fans, TV or the write-up in the paper. There was none of that. You played for the love of the game, the joy of competing and the ability to push yourself to be the best player possible.

At Iowa State, she then served as a graduate assistant during the 1985-1986 season. After graduate school, Goestenkors became an assistant coach at Purdue under head coach Lin Dunn. She helped assemble some of the best recruiting classes, including the country's top-rated squad in 1989. While at Purdue, she assisted the Boilermakers in reaching their record of 135–42, five consecutive 20-win seasons and five NCAA Tournaments which included two Sweet Sixteen appearances and Purdue's first Big Ten championship in 1991. The Associated Press final poll then ranked Purdue third in the nation. She also helped coach two Kodak All-American selections. Purdue's record when Goestenkors was on the coaching staff there was 148–68 (.685). Her ACC record at Duke was 69–43 through the 1998-99 season.

Goestenkors believes that she became a head coach because she had opportunity as a player and that opportunity made her very knowledgeable. "I was able to play, whether on a boys' team or a girls' team. I was able to play five on five, and it was a time when the men's TV package was really taking off. So not only did I get to play, but I got to watch and learn.

> I watched every game I could watch and listened. The announcers talked through the game, and I think that helped me become a better coach. Even when I was in college I coached a junior high team. I had so many wonderful experiences.

In her years at Duke, Goestenkors has had many firsts for the university. As 1996, 1998 and 1999 ACC Coach of the Year, she is Duke's only multiple winner of that honor and one of only two ACC coaches to earn it three times. In 1999 her team made the NCAA Final Four and appeared in the national championship game. Overall, she has coached Duke to five straight NCAA Tournaments, to four 20-plus win seasons over the last five years, to the most successful five-year stretch in the history of the program with 120 wins and 69 ACC victories and five NCAA bids, and to school record wins. In 1999, she led Duke to its best ACC finish in school history with a 15–1 conference mark.

While Goestenkors says that getting to the Final Four in 1999 and winning over Tennessee in a "kind of a David and Goliath type of a game" gave her an incredible feeling—as did being in the Final Four and beating Georgia, and getting to the championship—all outstanding achievements are not necessarily related to wins or losses:

> Other outstanding achievements are having all of my players graduate in four years. A lot of places it takes 4½ or 5 years to graduate. Just having all of them graduate in 4 years, I feel pretty proud about that. The thing I love most is working with the players in practice, and watching them learn and helping them grow. Over the course of four years, they come in girls and they leave women. Finding out what kind of women they are destined to become, and watching them not just over the four years, but then after that who they become—I derive a lot of pleasure in just watching people grow and helping them to grow.

Goestenkors' commitment to the varsity women's game is strong:

> I love the women's game, and we've come so far. It's exciting to be a part of the growth. I think we are very fortunate because we can see where the men have been and where they are now, and where they're going. We kind of have a model. I would like for us to take the positive. I don't think we want to become the men's game. I feel like the women's game is still very pure. I'm sure you've heard the quote from John Wooden, who is one of the greatest, if not the greatest coach of all time, the legendary coach at UCLA—who said he believed that the best women's teams right now play the best, most pure basketball: "I think the top women's college basketball teams, the very top teams, play the pure game better than the men do. I'm not saying they'd beat the men. They can't. But they play the pure game better ... devoid of physical power and showmanship." What he means by that is that [the men's game has] gotten to the point where it's just one on one, and it's just who can dunk the hardest. It's not a team game anymore where passing is important, where cutting and setting screens are, and where all five players work in unison. That's beauty, and the men have lost that. I want to learn from them; but we don't want to become them. We have such a wonderful game, and it is unique. I think that's what makes it special.

Goestenkors says that as the game continues to grow and as younger coaches strive for success she hopes they will keep the big picture in mind. She hopes each coach will do more than what's best for her and her program, and do what is best for women's basketball.

### ANGIE LEE[17]

As head coach of women's basketball at the University of Iowa, Angie Lee has kept Iowa's program a "perennial power." The honors Lee has accumulated in her four seasons are stellar. She has earned a record of 74–42 (.638). To what does Lee attribute her success?

> One of the biggest things that has made a difference in my life is a letter that my father gave to me and all of my brothers and sisters in 1977. He gave us a broom for Christmas, and with this broom was a letter. Basically what this letter talked about was if you ever

have to make brooms or anything like it, do it the best that you can and do it proudly. And he talked about what you sweep into your life and what you try to sweep out of your life. The background is that he had to give up something he loved, because he couldn't afford to do it anymore and he had to go make brooms, but that eventually led him to get back into what he loved, which was farming. So, that letter for me kind of entails what I try to do.

Angie Lee, head coach, women's basketball, University of Iowa.

Lee's parents, John and Jean Lee, are from Paxton, Illinois. She has two sisters and four brothers. She went to the University of Iowa, where she earned two degrees. In 1984, she earned a B.S., and in 1987 a master's degree in athletic administration.

As a student-athlete, Lee was a three-time Dean's List honoree. In 1982, she was Iowa's Defensive Player of the Year; in 1984, she was the team's All-Around team member and the Student-Athlete of the Year in the Department of Physical Education and Dance. In 1983-84, Lee was captain during coach Vivian Stringer's first season at Iowa. Iowa began to ascend as a power in the Big Ten.

Lee talks of her player experience in the position of point guard:

> It is an interesting position, because the point guard is the cog in the engine. The point guard is the one position that has to know all of the other positions. Without a doubt they have to know the other positions. They've got to know the strength and weaknesses of everybody on that team. Not to say that everybody shouldn't, but a point guard definitely does. I don't know that that has really changed in the game in that position.

In 1987-88 Lee served as the graduate assistant coach at Western Illinois. From 1989 to 1995, she was Vivian Stringer's assistant coach at Iowa. The players Lee recruited enabled Stringer and her staff to win four consecutive Big Ten titles (1989–1992) and play in five straight NCAA tournaments (1989–1994). In 1993-1994, she was elected to represent District IV assistant coaches at the WBCA. When Stringer left Iowa for Rutgers in 1995, Lee became head coach.

In her first four seasons as coach, Lee compiled a 74–42 (.638) record. Her team won two conference titles, a conference tournament title and two NCAA tournament berths. In her first season at Iowa, the Hawkeyes made it to the Sweet Sixteen following an 11–17 season. In 1996 she received four major honors: Big Ten Coach of the Year, Associated Press Division I Coach of the Year, Converse/WBCA District IV Coach of the Year, and College Sports Magazine Division I Coach of the Year. In 1997, Lee was a scout for the U.S. National Basketball Team during the twenty-sixth European championships in Budapest, Hungary, and the World Championships in Berlin, Germany.

Lee considers one of her most outstanding achievements the scholastic achievements of her 1998-1999 team:

> We had what you would consider a sub par season when you look at a 12 and 16 record, but we were a team that consisted of eight freshmen, two sophomores, and one senior. We had no juniors, so we were very young, but we got awarded the scholar team of the year with a 3.1 cumulative GPA, and that was very significant. As coaches, especially in the women's game, we try extremely hard to make kids understand we are student athletes, and that our education still has to be the biggest thing. I think when that [award] happened that was very exciting.

What does Lee say is her major contribution?

> I think it's basically the effort that is given every day to try to make a positive difference in young women's lives. You try every day to be an example for them, of how to continue to be persistent, to try to make the right choices, to do things the right way. I don't know that you ever get done contributing. I think the second that you think you are done contributing, you ought to hang it up to do something else to contribute somewhere else. I think what is important in coaching is

that we remember our contributions are never final, but they are always ongoing as long as you continue to touch young kids' lives.

Lee says, "My philosophy is always that your defense dictates your offense. On any given night, you can be stopped offensively, but you never have to be off defensively. You can always be on defensively. That is the kind of team that will continue to win you championships." And off the court, "I believe, like the university's academic community, that my mission is to inspire young women to extend their greatness and high goals beyond the realm of the basketball court."

Lee keeps her father's Christmas letter in a frame right beside her bed, so when she wakes up in the morning she sees it:

> To each of my kids, this year I am giving a new broom. A new broom sweeps clean. You may laugh and think the old man has been in the beer again, but I do want you to take a minute and think and contemplate what I have to say.
>
> Each of you is progressing beautifully and I am confident you will continue to prosper, but look at the broom and think of the workmanship which has been put into it. Remember if you ever have to make brooms or anything similar, do it proudly and do it well.
>
> I want each of you to take the broom and use it wisely. I want you to sweep from your life, jealousy, bickering, pride, the better-than-you some of us have.
>
> I want you to sweep into your life understanding, patience, forgiveness, love, and a better understanding of your God. With these things in order, you will experience peace of mind, happiness, confidence and fortitude to accomplish the things in life you desire. Learn to work in harmony with each other and your fellow man. Look for the bright side of everything—SMILE—and remember, "There is so much good in the worst of us and so much bad in the best of us so it ill behooves any of us to talk about the rest of us."
>
> God bless you all and Merry Christmas
> Dad

Lee says, "To me it's what life is, trying to make a difference. You know winning and losing, sometimes you're going to win, sometimes you're going to lose. It's all how you look at it. If you don't give up. I think there's as much to learn in losing as in winning, and I think success is relative. You've got to understand what your definition of success is."

## Nancy Lieberman-Cline[18]

Nancy Lieberman-Cline, the general manager and head coach of the Detroit Shock of the Women's National Basketball Association (WNBA), is one of the most accomplished and recognized players and coaches of women's basketball. She says of her long and multi-faceted basketball career, "Since I was 10 years old, no sport has ever been inside me the way basketball is—the decision making, the uncertainty of the game, the way you can't really predetermine what you are going to do because it is more read and react." From player to coach to broadcasting, she says that it is exciting to coach and to teach and share insight. "We are trying to make everyone a little bit better and a little bit more willing to do what's best for the good of the team and to help mold people. It is an awesome responsibility to be a coach, but I like it and I never thought I would. I really enjoy contributing on this side. There's nothing like playing, but the second-best thing is to be able to transform your players as a coach. It's the best of both worlds."

Lieberman-Cline's success in basketball demonstrates continuity, breadth and depth. She grew up in Brooklyn, New York, playing hoops on Harlem basketball courts. In high school she was a 5 foot 10 point guard. Her achievements began by the age of 15. She earned one of 12 slots on the USA's national team and was an All-American player every year. In 1975 she led the USA to a gold medal at the Pan American games. In 1976, she was named to the USA women's Olympic basketball team which competed in the Montreal games. At age 18, she became the youngest basketball player in Olympic history to win a medal as the United States won the silver.

Among her many honors as a player at Old Dominion University from 1976 to 1980 are three-time All-America, two-time winner of the Broderick Cup, and the only two-time Wade Trophy recipient. She led the ODU team to AIAW national championships. She scored 2,430 points, and had 1,167 rebounds, 983 assists and over 700 steals in her 134-game career.

Nancy played for four domestic professional leagues beginning in 1980-1981. She was chosen as the top draft pick by the Dallas Diamonds of the Women's Professional Basketball League (WBL). Some of her other professional accomplishments include being named MVP of the WABA All-Star Game; becoming the first female player in history to play in a men's league with the USBL Springfield Fame in 1986; and playing with the Washington Generals in 1987-1988 against the Harlem Globetrotters.

In 1996, she was inducted into the Naismith Memorial Basketball Hall of Fame as a player. In 1997, she played in the inaugural WNBA season for the Phoenix Mercury.

In 1998 she became the coach for the WNBA Detroit Shock and led her team to a 17–13 record. In 1999, she coached the Shock to a 15–17 record and made the WNBA playoffs. It was the first

Nancy Lieberman-Cline, general manager and head coach, Detroit Shock (WNBA).

time that a WNBA expansion team had qualified for the playoffs. Off the court, Nancy has been an analyst and commentator for ESPN and a guest columnist for *USA Today*.

In 1999, a newly created athletic award that honors the top collegiate point guard in women's basketball was named after Lieberman-Cline. In response, she said, "Recognizing the nation's top collegiate point-guard, while at the same time raising money for such an important cause as the American Cancer Society's fight against breast cancer, is extra special to me. I am grateful for the opportunity to play a role in this important cause."

In assessing the changes in the women's game, Nancy says, "The biggest change since the demise of the short shorts has to be the depth and quality of the players. With opportunity, with Title IX, with scholarships, and with TV, young girls are getting a chance to see what they can be." In response to the criticism that some players consider only the benefits of the game to them, she says, "I really have a hard time when people rip today's players by saying they don't care about the game, or they don't love it, or they are just playing for this or that. It's not their fault that they grew up in an era of having and wanting more." She says that there were most likely players in earlier days who didn't appreciate all that they had, but that, for the most part, players do appreciate the game and the fun of the game. She sees the style of coaching changing to one of allowing players to express themselves more.

### CHERYL LITTLEJOHN[19]

Cheryl Littlejohn, head coach at the University of Minnesota, says, "Kids need to know what they are getting into when they come here and so do their parents. I say that I'm only going to find out how successful I am as a coach twenty years from now, when I see how successful their child has become." To attain the goal of success, she believes in rigorous discipline for players, but as Britt Robson characterized her, "She insists the ends justify the means— and she isn't talking just about winning games." Littlejohn is a former player for successful Tennessee head coach Pat Summitt, and she is the daughter of Delores Littlejohn. Both women demanded disciplined hard work, inspired unwavering loyalty and conditioned Cheryl to succeed. Clearly Cheryl is herself a taskmaster, and loves a challenge.

Cheryl believes that coaching is the easiest part of her work. The more difficult part takes place in homes, gymnasiums and over phones all over the country. She is a dedicated recruiter who spends over three-quarters of her time checking on business related to her players, such as their majors and career opportunities. She researches museums and other places of interest before her team goes to a particular city.

Littlejohn, a native of Gastonia, North Carolina, considers her childhood "blessed," one in which she overcame obstacles through disciplined hard work. Her father died when she was seven, leaving her mother to rear the three children. At 14, along with her siblings, she worked in a service station and tutored peers at the local Boys Club to contribute to the family income. She was recruited for basketball by Florida State, Old Dominion, Notre Dame and Tennessee.

While earning her degree in criminal justice from the University of Tennessee, Littlejohn was a four-year letter winner from 1983 to 1987 and played on three Final Four teams, an SEC championship team and an NCAA national championship team in 1987, the first of five national titles for Summitt. In 1985 she won the Lady Vols Hustle Award and in 1987, the Gloria Ray Leadership Award. From 1987 to 1991, Littlejohn worked in the Drug Enforcement Administration in Los Angeles. In 1991, she became the first assistant coach at North Carolina State. She helped lead the team to the NCAA tournament in 1994. She scored her first top-10 recruiting class in her first year as an NCAA Division I basketball coach. Cheryl, a dedicated recruiter, would begin to get to know

Cheryl Littlejohn, head coach, women's basketball, University of Minnesota.

her recruits in the ninth and tenth grades. Her second recruiting class was rated by scouting services as among the top ten.

In 1995, Littlejohn became the first assistant coach and recruiting coordinator at the University of Alabama. While there, she helped the team make three NCAA Sweet Sixteen appearances and was ranked number two in the country in preseason polls in 1996-1997.

In 1997 Littlejohn became the women's head basketball coach at the University of Minnesota. Her 4–23 first season team was followed by a second season team with six newcomers and only three returning starters. Littlejohn knew it was a completely different team, and she told the press so: "Trust comes with stability, with knowing somebody. When you have a major transition, that's usually hard to get. This team made a commitment in the off season to do things together as a team.... Chemistry doesn't just show up every day in practice. You have to make the extra effort off the court. And that's exactly what they're doing." But she successfully coached her "new team" to a 7–20. At the end of the 1998-1999 season, her two season record at Minnesota was

11–42 (.204). In August of 1999, Littlejohn received the "Heroes in the Making" award from Minnesota Lynx and Jostens Company.

Littlejohn's formula for success leads to great results off and on the court: "Dedication, hard work and a commitment to excellence through teamwork will guarantee not only success on the court, but success in life."

### CHERYL MILLER[20]

"I always coached and played for the love of the game," says Cheryl Miller, head coach and general manager of the WNBA's Phoenix Mercury. The greatest satisfaction as a coach, she says, "is seeing players succeed on and off the court. Outstanding coaches are those coaches that not only make an impact on people's basketball skill but also on their personal lives. Living off the court is just as important as on the court."

While attending Polytechnic High School in Riverside, California, Miller became the first male or female to be named a Parade All-American four years straight and was named Street and Smith's Player of the Year in 1981 and 1982.

According to WNBA, "She was the first player to 'elevate' the women's game with her superior leaping ability." Her athletic skills were reflected by her earning All-America honors four consecutive years. Miller was a three-time College Player of the Year (1984–1986). She led the University of Southern California (USC) to two consecutive NCAA titles in 1983 and 1984. She earned honors three times as a member of the NCAA All-Tournament team and the two-time NCAA tournament MVP. She led the United States to its first Olympic gold medal in 1984. She was the only three-time Naismith Player of the Year, as well as a one-time Wade Trophy and Broderick Award winner. She was the first USC basketball player, male or female, to have her jersey retired.

In 1985, Miller was voted ESPN Woman Athlete of the Year. In 1986, she led the U.S. to titles in the World Championship of Basketball and the Goodwill Games, and she was the first woman basketball player to be nominated for the Sullivan Award (1986.)

In 1993 and 1994, Miller coached at USC, where she had a coaching record of 44–14 (.759). In 1994, USC won the Pacific-10 conference title. In 1995 Miller joined Turner Sports as an NBA reporter and analyst. In 1995 she was one of 11 women to have

Cheryl Miller, head coach and general manager, Phoenix Mercury (WNBA). (Photograph: Mitchell Lawton.)

been inducted into the Naismith Memorial Basketball Hall of Fame. In 1996, she became the first female analyst on a nationally televised NBA game. In 1999 she became a member of the first class of the Women's Basketball Hall of Fame.

Cheryl and her younger brother, Reggie, of the Indiana Pacers, are the greatest sister-brother basketball combination in history, according to the WNBA. In 1996, Reggie represented the U.S. at the Atlanta Olympics on the Dream Team.

In January 1997, Miller was named head coach and general manager of the WNBA's Phoenix Mercury. In the first year of the WNBA's existence, Miller, 36, led Phoenix to the playoffs and in 1999, into the finals. Miller's record is a 43–34 regular season record and a 13–4 record in the playoffs.

Miller's spectacular and consistent record demonstrates her ability to train a team to win, but she maintains, "Whether you are coaching men or women it is important to respect your players as people. Try to influence and make a difference in your players' lives on and off the court. It's the big picture that really counts."

## BILLIE MOORE[21]

Billie Moore, head coach at UCLA (1977–1993) and a women's basketball coach for 24 years, was elected to the Naismith Basketball Hall of Fame in October 1999. Earlier that year, in June she had been inducted into the Women's Basketball Hall of Fame in Knoxville, Tennessee. Moore was the first woman's coach to win AIAW national championships at two schools, California State at Fullerton in 1970 and the University of California at Los Angeles in 1978. She coached the first U.S. Olympic women's basketball team to a silver medal in Montreal in 1976.

In the 1950s, Moore's father was the high school principal and the coach of both boys' and girls' basketball teams in Westmoreland, Kansas. Moore says of her high school days, "I was very fortunate. It was such a small town that I didn't know girls weren't supposed to compete." Her family then moved to Topeka, where she attended Highland Park High School—which offered no sports for girls. "Girls were supposed to play for social purposes, says Moore, "but, by that time, the idea of playing to win was too ingrained in me for any of that to take."

In her early college coaching, she held coaching clinics because that was also the first year colleges went full-court. Moore, who had grown up playing boys' rules, says, "One woman actually asked me how you get the ball from one end of the court to the other. It gave me a bit of an edge."

From 1969 to 1977 at California State at Fullerton, she compiled a 140–15 (.903) record and led her teams to eight consecutive

Billie Moore, head coach, women's basketball (1977–1993), UCLA.

conference titles. In 1972 and 1975 her teams took third place in the national tournament. In 1971, her team finished fifth.

From 1977 to 1993 at UCLA she compiled a 296–181 (.621) record. Her overall record is 436–196 (.690). She led UCLA to the AIAW national title in 1978 and to a fourth place finish in 1979.

In 1993, Moore left UCLA, citing burnout as her reason. She

was the eighth coach in history to reach the 400 win mark. In 1973 and 1975 she was the head coach for USA World University team, and in 1975 she was an assistant coach for USA Pan-Am team.

At the time of her induction into the Hall of Fame in 1999, she said that the first thoughts she had "were of all the players, all the other people who had [been] a part of my coaching career."

In 1999, Moore is active in golf and works as a consultant to college and WNBA staffs, is a motivational speaker, and runs off-season WNBA camps.

### Rene Portland[22]

Rene Portland, head coach of women's basketball at Penn State, epitomizes multi-role success. A successful coach for over 20 years, she has incorporated a "family atmosphere" into the Penn State program. She uses her own successful life as a role model for her players. The mother of three and married 25 years, Rene says, "Exposing my athletes to a family situation has helped our team. Everybody depends on each other; everybody's loyal. I think the exposure of the family situation to our student athletes is very beneficial. They've been able to see you can juggle many things in life and still be successful." Portland says coaching her own daughter has given her the greatest satisfaction. "We are the only ones that lasted four years," she says, adding that in Division I, only one other mother and daughter have tried the coach-daughter relationship.

As a collegiate player at Immaculata under Coach Cathy Rush from 1972 to 1975, Rene helped her team win three national titles. She was awarded a New York Press All-American citation as a forward and center. Rush's teams were inducted into the Basketball Hall of Fame in 1974. Rene Portland gives us insight into Immaculata's excellence: "Three of us that played on that team are [successful] college coaches: Theresa Grentz, who is the head coach of the University of Illinois; Marianne Stanley, head coach at the University of California at Berkeley; and myself. Twenty-five years later to still be coaching successfully is pretty unique." After graduation, Portland became Rush's assistant coach, and that year, the Macs were the national runners-up to Delta State.

Through 1998-1999, Portland's teams won almost 75 percent of the games she coached (501–172, or .744). Her seasons include 21 at Penn State (1980–present), two at Colorado University

(1978–80), and two at St. Joseph's (1976–78). She has seven 25-win seasons and seventeen 20-win seasons. In March 1998, she led the Lady Lions to the Women's National Invitational tournament title and advanced to the championship game of the Big Ten Tournament for the third time, and her Penn State team posted 20 wins 14 times. In 1997, Portland achieved her four hundredth win at Penn State when, in the Big Ten opener, Penn upset No. 8 Wisconsin, 86–71. She became the ninth coach ever and the eighth active coach to reach her five hundredth career victory in the Women's National Invitational tournament semifinal win over Indiana.

Rene Portland, head coach, Lady Lion basketball, Pennyslvania State University.

Twice Portland has had victories in USA Basketball. In 1997, her U.S. junior national team won the gold medal for the first time ever at the world championships, upsetting defending champion Australia, 78–74. In 1996, her junior USA Basketball team received the silver medal at the world championship qualifying tournament in Chetumal, Mexico. In addition, her team won the silver medal at the World University Games in Palma de Mallorca, Spain.

Other coaching credits include 14 upsets of higher-ranked teams. Six of those wins came when Lady Lions had no standings in the national rankings. In 1988, the Lady Lions won 66–62 over Louisiana Tech, then number 2.

Portland has coached one of only six teams that has 14 NCAA appearances. Her teams have won 20 or more games 14 times during her 18 seasons, and in 8 of the last 9 seasons. She has reached the 20-victory mark 17 times in her 22 years.

Portland's emphasis on teamwork also develops top individual athletes. Lady Lion Susan McConnell became a two time

Olympian (1988, 1992). All-American player Susan Robinson was awarded the 1992 Wade Trophy.

Portland says that she has been "at it" a long time, first as a player; then, "I proceeded to coach through the growth of women's athletics and have maintained a standard of academic as well as athletic standards." She adds, "I'm very outspoken on Title IX." She is also very active in the Women's Basketball Coaches Association and served as its president during the 1989-1990 season. "I've served on many, many committees besides doing what most coaches do, winning and losing. I have coached USA teams, and really gone beyond to make sure that the growth of our sport does happen. I'm very outspoken on gender equity." She has also been active on "Rene's List," a fund-raising effort that assists with the production of televised games of several women's sports. She was one of 10 women's coaches invited by the National Basketball Association to discuss the future of women's professional leagues in the United States. On May 9, 1995, Portland and WBCA second vice president Sylvia Hatchell, head coach of women's basketball for Olympic sports at the University of North Carolina, Chapel Hill, represented WBCA and met with members of Congress during Title IX hearings to protect opportunities for women and girls in sport. In 1994, she was voted Coach of the Year by the Big Ten coaches. Twice in the period of 1992–1999, she was recognized as the National Coach of the Year. In 1995, she was a Naismith finalist.

That she coached her own daughter, Christine, remains her greatest satisfaction. "My daughter not only sat on the bench on my team as a freshman, but was a starter her junior and senior year and was captain of our basketball team in 1998-1999. The fact that she chose and played on a top 20 basketball program and did very, very well was very satisfying for the mother as well as the coach." Portland compares her daughter's experience with her own student days at Immaculata College, when there were three national champions before Title IX had any effect, before scholarships and before all those benefits available to players now. She is grateful to see her daughter having opportunities not available in her day: "I saw someone then, receive a scholarship in the same blood line and get everything that I didn't get 20 some years ago in college. It is very neat to watch all of that happen and be part of it."

Portland imparts her family values to her players with the phrase she has used to inspire her team for as long as she has been playing: "Remember who you are and what we represent." That's important, Portland says. "Sometimes, we forget that and become selfish. You always have to remember you're part of the team, and who you represent is now your team and your university. This whole experience is bigger than yourself. And you have to remember that. When you remember that then you can do a great job for everybody around you."

### Marianne Stanley[23]

Marianne Stanley, the head coach at the University of California since 1996, is one of the most successful and yet one of the most controversial coaches in college basketball. In the 1970s and 1980s she coached Old Dominion University to three AIAW national titles. At 24, she was the youngest NCAA Division I women's basketball coach to guide her team to a national championship. She has earned four Conference Coach of the Year honors and National Coach of the Year recognition twice. Her record is an impressive 404–207 (.661) through the 1998-1999 season. In her 20 years as a head coach, she is tied for twenty-sixth in victories among all active NCAA Division I women's head coaches. In 1999, at home against Arizona State (74–60), she tied as the twelfth-youngest coach, at age 44, to hit the 400-win plateau.

As a player at Immaculata College, Pennsylvania, Stanley was a two-time All-America guard and led her team to four consecutive AIAW national championship games from 1973 to 1976. The team won the AIAW national championship in 1973 and 1974.

From 1987–1989, Stanley coached at the University of Pennsylvania. Her record there was 11–41. In 1989 she became coach at the University of Southern California. Stanley took her USC team to three NCAA tournaments, including an Elite Eight appearance in 1992. She coached at USC until 1993 and had a record of 71–46. In her 1995-1996 year at Stanford she earned a record of 29–3 and appeared at the NCAA Final Four. Her three years at the University of California at Berkeley earned her a record of 24–58.

Stanley's national team coaching record is 47–13 with 10 different U.S. teams.

From 1989 to 1993, Stanley coached at the University of Southern California. In 1993, Stanley demanded a raise from $62,000

Marianne Stanley, head coach, women's basketball, University of California–Berkeley.

to $130,000, to equal the base salary of the men's coach, George Raveling. She filed an $8 million sex discrimination suit against the university. In September 1993, the University of Southern California fired Marianne Stanley. In response to the university's action, Betty Jaynes, the executive director of the Women's Basketball Coaches Association, said, "The discriminatory actions taken by USC send the wrong signal to other women's coaches who may want to pursue their right to equal pay for equal work. The WBCA wholeheartedly supports Coach Stanley."

While Stanley fought her legal battles, USC was going against a trend. Other prominent coaches such as the University of Washington's Chris Gobrecht, the University of Iowa's Vivian Stringer, Tennessee's Pat Summitt, Gooch Foster of Cal, Tara VanDerveer of Stanford, Gary Blair of the University of Arkansas and Debbie Ryan of the University of Virginia were provided base salaries equal or nearly equal to those of their counterparts coaching the men's teams.

Despite her outstanding achievements in basketball, Stanley was out of a coaching job from 1993 to 1995 while her case made its way through the legal system. In 1993 she took a job stripping and sanding furniture in a Los Angeles upholstery store. The work was what she needed to ease her difficult time. Stanley said, "Stripping furniture is nasty work. It was an outlet at the time because I could sweat, step back and be alone. None of the other guys at the shop spoke English, which is exactly what I wanted because I didn't have to explain myself or what I felt to anybody." In 1994 she took a part-time marketing job with Stanford basketball. She did not attend the Stanford game against USC because it was "too painful."

From 1993 to 1995, Stanley applied for "approximately 100" head coaching jobs, but she did not receive any offers. In 1995, she was working a book cataloguing job in South Carolina. Then, when Tara VanDerveer at Stanford accepted an offer to coach the 1996 Olympic team, Stanley was offered the opportunity to become the co–head coach at Stanford with VanDerveer's assistant, Amy Tucker. She accepted the position and coached at Stanford for a year.

In the fall of 1996, Stanley became head coach of women's basketball at the University of California. There, her starting base salary was the same as the men's coach, $110,000 a year. Stanley's response in 1996: "I've always wondered if one person can make a difference. And I've found out first hand that you can."

Stanley's struggle benefitted other coaches. In 1996, about 27 NCAA Division I-A women's basketball coaches received new contracts or extensions paying in excess of $100,000 a year in base salary equal to or even more than the men's coaches at their schools.

Although in 1996, Stanley said that one of the last things she could ever imagine herself doing was filing a lawsuit, she concluded, "I don't just coach basketball. Part of coaching on the university level—on any level—is being an educator. Hopefully, basketball is a vehicle to teach some much broader lessons about life. In a huge way, that's what this lawsuit is about. It's much bigger than Marianne Stanley. It's much bigger than basketball. It's about ethics and values and fairness. They're bigger than everybody."

But in June 1999, Stanley received a setback in her equal pay case. The Ninth U.S. Circuit Court of Appeals, in a 2–1 decision, ruled in Southern California's favor, saying that it was all right for USC to pay Raveling more in part because he had more experience.

### BARBARA STEVENS[24]

In 1999 Bentley College said about head coach Barbara Stevens' accomplishments, "Over the past 13 years, very few college basketball coaches—at any level, men's or women's—can match the success achieved by Barbara Stevens since her arrival at Bentley College in September 1986." But Stevens says, "I look at achievements not so much in terms of wins and losses, but more in the sense of the people as opposed to the numbers, and would like to feel as though achievements in our program are ongoing and that our goal is to produce good people who will be positive citizens once they leave Bentley College and will be the best that they can be as contributors in society."

Stevens gets the most satisfaction in seeing her players graduate and go on to become successful young women. She says that it is "in our teaching moments" that coaches need to take advantage because "people do look at things you say and things you do and how you approach situations. It does have an effect on the young people that we work with, more so than I really ever realized."

Stevens says that the opportunities in the game have improved tremendously. "Young girls have more opportunities to compete, opportunities to learn, various activities in which they can learn the game, more so than when I was a young kid. [Back then] it was pretty much in the backyard with a parent, or a sibling, and now there are many more organized activities for young kids that allow them the opportunity to develop their skills." Stevens says "just the funding" alone is tremendously better.

Stevens, a point guard in college, played for four years at Bridgewater State College in Massachusetts. "Those of

Barbara Stevens, head coach, women's basketball, Bentley College.

us who were interested in sports did play, but in front of very few people and with very little fanfare and very little notice. How we practiced, the amount of time and what we did to get ready for a season are just so different now."

In 1976, Stevens began her coaching career as an assistant coach at Clark. In 1977, she was promoted to head coach. She won almost 75 percent of her games during her six seasons. The Cougars averaged better than 20 wins a season and reached the NCAA Division III Final Four in both 1982 and 1983. She guided her teams at Clark to three Division III state championships and five straight postseason tournaments. While at Clark she also served as softball coach coordinator of women's athletics and assistant athletic director. She was named District I Converse/WBCA Coach of the Year and coached the Division III Champion Player of the Year, Margie O'Brien.

In 1986, Stevens had accumulated a three-year record of 34–49 at the University of Massachusetts. She was a member of the

NCAA Division III Women's Basketball Committee from 1980 to 1983, and a member of the NCAA Basketball Rules Committee.

In 1994 Stevens was an assistant coach for the USA Select Team, traveling to France and Israel. In 1993, she was an assistant coach for the West in the Olympic Festival.

In 1999, Stevens in her thirteenth season at Bentley College had compiled a record 529 wins, the most ever by a Division II women's basketball coach. Her Bentley record stood at 372–54 (.873). Her teams were ranked in the top four nationally in Division II in each poll from 1991 to 1993. Her February 6, 1999, victory over Merrimack made her the winningest women's college basketball coach in Division II history at 520–145, surpassing the late Darlene May (Cal Poly Pomona, 519) for the top spot on the all-time Division II win list.

Stevens has led her team to six appearances in the NCAA Division II Fab Four, including five straight in 1989–93 and an appearance in the 1990 national championship game. Seven 30-win seasons with five in a row in 1989–93 gave her a record of better than 28 wins per season. She also led her team to 13 straight appearances in the NCAA Division II tournament, with nine regional championships, and eleven Northeast-10 regular season championships, breaking the school record for consecutive wins six times.

In 1994-1995, Stevens served as president of the WBCA, the only Division II coach to have done so. Other honors Stevens has earned are 1992 Converse/WBCA Division Coach of the Year, 1999 Ikon/WBCA Division II Coach of the Year, 1988-1989 American Women's Sports Federation Division II Coach of the Year, WBCA/Converse District I Coach of the Year from 1991 to 1993 and again in 1998-1999, and the Northeast-10 Conference Coach of the Year eight times (1988, 1989, 1991, 1992, 1993, 1996, 1997 and 1998).

The game changes, says Stevens, but

> in terms of coaching sometimes some of your biggest changes occur in terms of the athletes that you deal with. Society has changed. The way that you relate to your players is as important as the information that you give to them; and how you give it is probably more important. You have to have a good communication method these days. One of our basic principles of coaching philosophy is you must reach the athlete as a person first and then you can coach the athlete. That's the most important way we deal with approaching the people on our team.

Stevens would not like to see the game remain necessarily the same in terms of skill level. She hopes that it continues to improve and that women continue to grow and develop and get to be the best athletes that they can possibly be within the sport to showcase women's basketball. But she adds:

> I do hope that the sport remains somewhat pure and is an arena in which people can look at women's basketball and say, "Hey, that's how we want sport to be in America." For example, I think you look at women's soccer and what the U.S. women's soccer team did for the sport of women's soccer, it energized an entire country; it took the attention of the whole world in a very positive way. The young women were role models and I think they understood that, and I think they were watched closely for the entire time that they were going through the tournament.

Stevens considers herself fortunate. "I have a love for this sport and for this profession. I count my blessings"—because, she says, "coaching is a profession that you put your heart and soul into and you can't do it half-heartedly."

## C. VIVIAN STRINGER, HEAD COACH[25]

In the 1960s, Stringer played football and basketball. She describes her experience to *Sports Illustrated* as follows "I'd beat the boys during the week, but on Fridays they were the ones who got to wear the uniforms. There were no teams for girls. I found cheerleading frustrating because I could see how plays should have been executed or how a player should have scored, and I wanted to run out and show them."

Born in Edenborn, Pennsylvania, Stringer is a member of the Alumni Hall of Fame at her alma mater, Slippery Rock State College, where she studied physical education. Stringer and the late William D. Stringer have three children. Stringer's father was a coal miner, and her mother is currently employed at JC Penney's.

Stringer attributes her success, in part, to the strength of her father, who at a young age was disabled by arterial disease. His legs were amputated below the knee in two operations one year apart. Stringer told *Sports Illustrated,* "I remember hearing the moaning from behind closed doors, but we never heard him complain, and he kept working. Whenever I feel exhausted, I think of

Vivian Stringer, head coach, women's basketball, Rutgers, the State University of New Jersey. (Photograph: Larry Levanti.)

my dad and he gives me strength." Stringer applied this stalwart philosophy when she faced the illness of her young daughter, the death of her husband, and the responsibilities of single parenting.

Stringer did volunteer coaching for the women's teams during her first teaching job at Cheyney State College (now Cheyney University) in 1971. She built a basketball power without any scholarships, held bake sales to pay for uniforms and solicited churches to pay for letter sweaters. Stringer's teams, playing in Division I against schools 10 times the size of Cheyney, had an outstanding 251–51 record. In 1982, Stringer brought Cheyney State to the NCAA Final Four. In 1983, she landed the head coach position at Iowa. In 1993, she brought Iowa to the Final Four. In 1995, Stringer signed a contract with Rutgers that was reported to be a record-breaker, making her the top earner not only among all Rutgers coaches but in her entire field.

Stringer is the only women's coach to lead two different colleges (Cheyney State and the University of Iowa) to the Final Four. Both the Metropolitan Writers' Association and the New Jersey Basketball Coaches Association named Stringer Coach of the Year for the consecutive seasons 1997-98 and 1998-99. She was Coaches' Coach of the Year in 1993, 1988, and 1985, and Big Ten Coach of the Year, 1993 and 1991.

In her 27 years of coaching, Stringer has taken 13 teams to the NCAA tournament, including two Final Four trips and four regional finals. Third all-time winningest Division I coach in women's basketball with a career record of 595–183, she is the second youngest, and one of five active coaches to earn 500 career victories (January 28, 1994).

After 11 seasons at Cheyney State, Stringer amassed a 251–51 record. She raised the University of Iowa Hawkeyes from last in the Big Ten conference standings to the top of the nation's polls in five years. Iowa had 10 consecutive 20-win seasons, and nine straight NCAA tournament berths and won six Big Ten titles.

In 1981, 1983 and 1993 Stringer had the nation's best defensive team, and in 1985, she had the second-best defensive team. Her teams were the Pennsylvania AIAW state champions consecutively from 1979 to 1982.

In 1998-99, Stringer brought the Scarlet Knights' season to a close with a 29–6 record and finished in the Elite Eight of the NCAA tournament. They shared the Big East conference crown and ranked sixth in the nation in the *USA Today* coaches poll.

Stringer has received many awards. In 1999, she was the Metropolitan Writers Association Coach of the Year and a Naismith National Coach finalist. In 1998, she won awards from WBCA District I, Big East, the New Jersey Basketball Coaches Association, the Black Coaches Association, and the Metropolitan Writer's Association. In 1994 she was Giant Steps Female Coach. In 1993, she was honored by the Big Ten Conference Sportswriters, USA Today National, Naismith National, Carol Eckman Award, and Black Coaches Association National. Both 1993 and 1991 saw her honored by the Big Ten conference. In 1993 and 1988, she was Converse Division I, Sports Illustrated National Women's Coach. Other awards came in 1982 (NCAA); 1993, 1988, 1985 (NCA District V); 1983 (NCAA District II); 1982 (Pennsylvania AIAW); and 1981, 1980 (Philadelphia Sportswriters).

Stringer has received many other honors, including: the 1998 National Association of Negro Business and Professional Women's Club (Union Co.) Woman of the Year; the Jackie Robinson Award by the NAACP of New Brunswick; in 1998, the City News 100 Most Influential Award; in 1994, Iowa City Magazine's Person of the Year, Reggie McKenzie Foundation Commitment to Character Award; in 1993, Joe Cipriano/Jim Valvano Nike Hall of Fame; in 1991, coach, U.S. Pan American Games team; in 1989, coach, U.S. World Championship Zone qualification team; in 1987, inductee, Communiplex Hall of Fame; in 1985, coach, World University

Games; in 1982, coach, National Sports Festival East Team. She was an honoree for the Smithsonian Institution for Black Women in Sports, appeared in Who's Who Among Black Americans, and in 1980 she was coach for the U.S. Select Team (China Tour), Coach, Parade All-America South Team.

Stringer's philosophy, as Claire Smith of the *New York Times* reported in 1995 when Stringer first came to Rutgers, reflects her total energizing force: "I didn't come to rest." "I can't handle anything less than a high level of competitiveness and a great deal of success." Her intensity was shown in one of her other first statements, "I only intend to start over for a short period of time," she said. "I intend to jump right back up there where I had been." Later, in 1997, her words to *Sports Illustrated* echoed that winning drive: "The sickness I feel when we lose is a lot more intense than the exhilaration I feel in victory. However, I will pay the price. A lot of people want to achieve success, but only a few are willing to pay the price."

## PAT SUMMITT[26]

University of Tennessee's women's head basketball coach Pat Summitt is one of the most longstanding successful coaches. She has earned Coach of the Year honors four times. Her overall record at the end of 24 seasons at Tennessee was 644–143 (.818). Before her coaching career began, Summitt led the Lady Pacers of the University of Tennessee-Martin to a 64–29 (.688) record over four years. In 1976 she was the co-captain of the silver medal Olympic team, 1975 world championship team, 1975 U.S. national team to Taiwan, 1975 gold medal Pan American Games team and the 1973 silver medal U.S. World University Games team. Summitt has been compared to John Wooden, who established a standard of excellence in men's college basketball at UCLA. An Associated Press article calls her "the closest thing the women's game has to a wizard."

According to *Successful Farming* magazine, Summitt developed her skills as a fierce competitor in the hayloft of the family barn where she and her three brothers did "basketball battle" after the chores were done. The family unit instilled teamwork and hard work ethics that she holds for her athletes today.

These ethics are expressed in her recent book *Reach for the Summit*:

[I'm] someone who will push you beyond all reasonable limits. Someone who will ask you to not just fulfill your potential, but to exceed it. Someone who will expect more from you than you may believe you are capable of. So if you aren't ready to go to work, shut this book.

Summitt stresses throughout her book that every person is capable of her own brand of success, but she offers her own philosophy of success around a set of ethics and winning, and winning more than once. She proposes that "winners are not born, they are *self-made*," and that players must take ownership of their team and make a commitment to it. "If

Pat Summitt, head coach, Lady Vols basketball, the University of Tennessee. (Photograph: The Photography Center, University of Tennessee.)

you fail, it hurts so deeply. If you never make that commitment–if you just stand around waiting for things to happen–failure won't affect you so much. You think, *It's not my fault.* But you won't succeed either." Although Summitt is known for being tough on her players, her players know it is because she cares. She teaches things that help them for the rest of their lives. Summitt introduces every team to her "Definite Dozen," one by one:

1. Respect Yourself and Others
2. Take Full Responsibility
3. Develop and Demonstrate Loyalty
4. Learn to Be a Great Communicator
5. Discipline Yourself So No One Else Has To
6. Make Hard Work Your Passion
7. Don't Just Work Hard, Work Smart

8. Put the Team Before Yourself
9. Make Winning an Attitude
10. Be a Competitor
11. Change Is a Must
12. Handle Success Like You Handle Failure

Because Summitt has won so consistently, her concluding point, "Handle Success Like You Handle Failure," is important to capture. Summitt says that failure is hard to swallow, but easier to remedy, and that success is "a much trickier matter. It's like balancing on top of a pole. It's one thing to climb a pole, but quite another to stay up there. That's why it is so difficult to go undefeated. Your attention wanders, your original priorities become obscured, other people try to knock you off the top of the pole. Pretty soon you have lost your balance." In this context Summitt's ultimate wish for her players is a broader success than the one they experience at Tennessee, because success is a lifelong endeavor that eventually must be self-motivated.

### TARA VANDERVEER[27]

Tara VanDerveer, head coach at Stanford since 1986, has always retained her strong collegiate basketball ethic. In a 1996 *Sports Illustrated* article, VanDerveer said that a good university experience is related to an unwavering work ethic and success. Part of her coaching role is to push people out of their comfort zone. *Sports Illustrated* noted that VanDerveer once described her coaching philosophy in one word: work. When asked to elaborate, she said, 'Hard work.'" Her recruiting style reflects her understanding of intervarsity athletics: "I want people who can shoot, play defense and are in shape. I think there is a correlation between good students and work ethic." A particular team may not be "the most athletic team," but will be the best conditioned because it will outwork everybody else.

In 1995, VanDerveer took a year away from Stanford to coach the 1996 U.S. women's Olympic basketball team. One of the reasons she was content to then return to college basketball was that "the landscape of women's athletics is changing so much. There are a lot of different opportunities now."

In her book, *Shooting from the Outside: How a Coach and Her Olympic Team Transformed Women's Basketball*, VanDerveer says that going against convention did not bother her. Her father became the first male teacher in the history of Melrose, Massachusetts. "My parents instilled confidence and independence in all their children, encouraging us to navigate our way through decisions and prepare for the consequences." Her parents' teachings may account for VanDerveer's excellence as an X and O coach. Her father told her, "Have a good strategy. Nothing pops up tomorrow unless you plan for it."

In spite of her father's instruction, she says she had no plans as a child to become a basketball coach. Van-Derveer was born in Boston, but when living in West Hill, New York, the family was active in skiing, sailing, swim-

Tara VanDerveer, head coach, Stanford women's basketball, Stanford University.

ming, hiking, tossing the football, playing tetherball and basketball in the yard and participating in local YMCA hoop shooting. In the neighborhood basketball games, she played only when the boys needed another person to even their teams. But in the eighth grade as she stood on the periphery, she wondered: "Why do I have to watch? Why aren't I down there? Why do I like basketball so much?"

VanDerveer characterizes the players of her day as not having organized basketball until they got to college. Then all they had was sneakers they paid for themselves, uniforms they washed themselves, and a passion they nurtured themselves. In the early 1970s, Title IX was passed to address the imbalance in which a typical Big Ten conference school spent $1,300 on men's athletics for every dollar spent on women's.

VanDerveer graduated in 1975 from Indiana University. She

was a Dean's List scholar for three years and majored in sociology. As a basketball player at Indiana, VanDerveer was a starting guard. In 1995, she was named to the Indiana University Hall of Fame.

From 1978 to 1980 VanDerveer served as head coach at the University of Idaho. From 1980 to 1985, she led the Ohio State women's basketball team to four Big Ten championships, compiled four consecutive 20-win seasons and made two postseason appearances. In 1984-1985, Ohio State finished seventh in the national rankings and was runner-up to eventual national champion Old Dominion.

In 13 seasons at Stanford, VanDerveer coached the Cardinals to five Final Four appearances in eight years and two NCAA titles in 1990 and 1992. Her Stanford record through the 1998-1999 season is 306–70 (.814) and her Pac-10 record is 169–22 (.885). Her record in 19 years of college coaching is 458–121 (.791) and in seven basketball coaching assignments her record is 88–8 (.917). In 1999, VanDerveer ranked fourth in winning percentage among active Division I women's basketball coaches. Her 458 victories place her 17th among active coaches.

Among VanDerveer's many honors are Big Ten Coach of the Year in 1983-1984 and 1984-1985; National Coach of the Year in 1987-88, 1988-89, 1989-90; and USA Basketball National Coach of the Year in 1996. She was also named the 1996 USOC Elite Basketball Coach of the Year. She was inducted into the Women's Sports Foundation Hall of Fame in 1998.

In 1996 she served as head coach of the U.S. Olympic gold medal team in Atlanta. The team started its training in 1995 and won 60 straight games. VanDerveer shares her coaching philosophy of making this team a success in her book. She emphasizes the importance of communication: "Don't make your players guess what you're trying to tell them. Lay your cards on the table. Tell the truth as clearly as you know it."

In her book, she says, "Success is rooted not only in confidence and hard work but in joy. Passion produces its own energy. Women in sports are free now to embrace their passion for basketball and volleyball and track and field without reservation, without fear of being considered strange. We can throw everything we have into coaching and playing, which is the only path to excellence. I'm reminded of a remark the writer Pearl S. Buck once made. 'The secret of joy in work is contained in one word—excellence. To know how to do something well is to enjoy it.'"

### MARGARET WADE[28]

Margaret Wade graduated from Cleveland High School in her home state of Mississippi in 1929. She was an All-Conference player in 1928 and 1929. She played basketball three years at Delta State from 1930 to 1933. In 1930–1932, she was captain of her team and was All-Conference. In 1931-32 she was the team's most valuable player.

"Because it was deemed too strenuous for women," the women's basketball program at Delta State was abolished in 1933, notes the Naismith Hall of Fame biography of Margaret Wade. Wade and her teammates cried and burned their uniforms.

Wade played amateur basketball for the Mississippi Tupelo Red Wings. She was the team captain from 1934 to 1935 and led her team to the Southern Championship. A knee injury ended her playing career in 1935.

Upon graduation from Delta State in 1933, she began her high school coaching career in Mississippi at Marietta High School. Her record was 12–2. In 1934-35, she coached at Belden High School and had a record of 11–3. From 1935 to 1954, she coached at Cleveland High School and had a record of 453–89.

Wade became the first director of Delta State's women's physical education department in 1959, a position she held until 1973. That year, she reinstated the women's basketball program— which had been dormant for

Margaret Wade, head coach, women's basketball (1973–1979), Delta State University.

41 years—and became its head coach. Her first team's record was 16–2. From 1975 to 1977 she led her teams to three AIAW national championships with a 93–4 record that included a 51-game winning string. When Wade retired in 1979, she had compiled a 157–23 record.

In 1978, a trophy was named in her honor. It is presented each year to the top women's collegiate player. Wade was the first woman to be inducted into the Mississippi Sports Hall of Fame (1974) and Delta State University Hall of Fame. She is also enshrined in the Mississippi Coaches Hall of Fame.

By 1985, Wade concluded basketball had come a long way since she played in a gym that was divided into three zones and only bounce passes were allowed. ("I guess they thought if we threw the ball at another girl we'd hit her in the head.") Wade was elected to the Naismith Hall of Fame in 1985. She considered her election into the hall a great victory: "I guess maybe I had hopes, but I didn't really think they would ever put a woman in the Hall of Fame."

### MARIAN WASHINGTON[29]

When Marian Washington, head coach at the University of Kansas, reached the 500th victory mark in 1999, she had trouble expressing her feelings about her success—but not about players. "It's hard to say all of the things you feel. But it's really all about finding players. I've been fortunate to have some wonderful kids." The pressure to win is always there, but Washington is dedicated to producing a well-rounded student athlete as well. Teaching is the root of the collegiate coaching.

Washington grew up in West Chester, Pennsylvania. She was raised to be competitive and excelled in seven sports at Henderson High School. She participated in AAU basketball and competed internationally in the Soviet Union in basketball and in Canada in team handball.

At West Chester State College, her team won the first women's national basketball championship and won the National Women's Invitational tournament in 1969. That same year, she was one of the first two black women to make a United States national team. In 1970, she graduated with a B.A. degree in physical education and health. In 1972, she was a graduate assistant in the health, physical education and recreation department at West Chester. In

1975, she earned her M.A. degree in biodynamics and administration.

In 1973, Washington became head coach at Kansas. During her time there, scholarships have grown from zero to 15. Her overall record is 503–277 (.645). In conference play, Washington has a 159–85 (.652) record. Her postseason totals are 46–29 (.614). She has led her teams to 10 NCAA tournaments, two WNIT appearances and the AIAW Central Sectional tournament four times. Her teams have won six Big Eight (now Big Twelve) postseason tournament titles, the most of any conference

Marian Washington, head coach, women's basketball, University of Kansas.

school. Washington ranks eleventh among Division I's winningest active college coaches and is the fifth active coach to win 500 games at one school. She has had 20 winning seasons in the last 26 years.

In 1996, Washington became an assistant coach on the Olympic coaching staff. With the Women's Dream Team, Washington won the gold medal in Atlanta. Following her Olympic contribution, she was named William I. Koch Outstanding Woman of the Year.

Her many honors include, in 1996, the Big Eight Coach of the Year and the Black Coaches Association Coach of the Year. In 1995, she won the Giant Steps Award for giving her utmost to provide the support necessary for young people to fully realize their academic and athletic potential. In 1992, she was named the Black Coaches Association (BCA) Women's Coach of the Year, Big Eight Conference Coach of the Year and the Kansas Basketball Coaches Association Women's Coach of the Year. From 1993 to 1994, she was the first female to serve as president of the Black Coaches

Association and the first female to serve in consecutive terms. In 1995, she was one of 10 athletes inducted into the West Chester State Women's Athletic Hall of Fame.

Washington came to Kansas to build a program and said of her 500th win, "I am most proud of the fact that we have a wonderful reputation for men's basketball. And now we have a wonderful history and tradition for women's." She is known as a patient coach who listens. Washington says, "I think when you're an athlete, you can't fathom that day when you're not going to play. It's hard when you're young to see that far ahead. But I always loved teaching."

### KAY YOW[30]

Kay Yow, head basketball coach for women at North Carolina State, began her 25th year there with the start of the 1999-2000 season. Her record for 24 years is 512–214 (.710). Her overall record as a collegiate head coach for 28 years is 552–221 (.714). In 1996, she earned her 500th career win and in 1998 she won her 500th game at North Carolina State.

As a "player's coach," she mentors and guides while assuming the role of mother for players away from home. She schedules meetings to talk about basketball and life. She sends every former player a Christmas card and a birthday card with a personal note.

Kay Yow is a Christian with a strong faith. She says, "The way I relate to people is governed a lot by my faith. The way I go about doing everything is related to that, because that's my foundation as a person. I believe it impacts my interpersonal relationships and my people skills. My motivation for everything I do originates from my faith." She also believes that motivating talented players to become a winning team requires chemistry and hard work: "Chemistry takes time and it comes from within the people themselves. It is a lot about understanding and accepting roles. That involves people skills as much as it does basketball skills. We just have to work with players in all areas and continue to grow as people as well as basketball players to have the kind of chemistry we would like."

Yow coached at the high school level before entering the collegiate level. At Allen Jay High School from 1964 to 1968, her four year record was 77–20 (.794), and at Gibsonville High School from 1969 to 1970, her one year record was 15–7 (.682). From 1974 to 1975 she coached at Elon College for four years and produced a record of 57–19 (.750). Her North Carolina State teams were NCAIAW champions and have been participants in AIAW and NCAA tournaments. The Wolfpack women have been Regular Season ACC Champions 5 times and ACC Tournament Champions 4 times.

Yow graduated from East Carolina College in 1964. She has said she always felt like something was missing in her college experience. In those years women's basketball was not yet a varsity sport at East Carolina, nor had Title IX been passed.

Kay Yow, head coach, women's basketball, North Carolina State.

Yow is proud of the strides that women's basketball has made. She says, "I can't believe that we are where we are. When I think back to high school, I never imagined women's basketball being fully scholarshipped at the college level and being played professionally."

In November 1999, she was inducted into the Women's Basketball Hall of Fame. Her many awards include, in 1998, College Sports News Women's Basketball Coach of the Year.

On the international level she has an overall record of 21–1 (.955). In the 1981 World University Games, she coached the United States team to a 4–1 record and the silver medal. In the 1988 Olympics, the United States team were 5–0 and won the gold medal. In 1986 world championships, she coached the United States team to a 7–0 record and the gold medal and in the 1986 Goodwill Games her team went undefeated (5–0) and won the gold.

Yow says what it takes to keep the upper edge, to be top notch year after year, is great talent, great people surrounding you, and solid coaching. "A great team is usually the result of many factors coming together," she says, "I'm fortunate at NC State to have such an outstanding support staff as well as coaching staff. This enables everyone to strive to be their best."

## A Final Word

The coaches profiled represent what is best in women's college basketball. They are but a few of the hundreds of women who have changed the game, made it grow, and contributed to the development of thousands of student athletes, some of whom followed them into the coaching profession.

# Chapter 6

# *The Coaches and the Future*

*"What visions, what expectations and what presumptions can outsoar that flight?"*

Kahlil Gibran

From the time of the first women's basket ball game just before the beginning of the twentieth century to the phenomenal growth and popularity of women's basketball at the start of the twenty-first century, the guiding force has been the coaches. The women (and men) who coach the game have provided and continue to provide a rich legacy. The early college teams were coached by women and still the majority of teams have women coaches, but today more men are guiding women's teams.

The impact of Title IX on women's athletics in general and women's basketball in particular was tremendous. Coach after coach tells the story of what it was like to play and coach before 1972 when Title IX was passed. They played for the love of the game—and still do, but today they are able to play it on a more level playing field. The number of scholarships, money for recruiting, funds for operating expenses, and numbers and salaries of coaches are, in too many cases, still weighted heavily in favor of the men's programs, but the tide is moving in the direction of equity

159

and it will continue to do so in the 21st century. The forces loosed by Title IX will not be turned back, but it will take continued vigilance and efforts by women in all facets of the sport to make sure that the move toward equity continues unabated.

As the women's game moves into the 21st century, the spirit and skill of the coaches will continue to provide players who elevate the game to new heights in the quality of play. Their accomplishments have sparked a dramatic growth in interest in the game. The number of colleges playing women's basketball and the number of people who attend the games will continue to grow.

The development and expansion of the WNBA attests to the quality of the players these coaches produce. The WNBA offers opportunity for women coaches in college to move to the professional level and to contribute to the growth of the game by so doing.

The number of elementary, junior high and high school girls who are playing basketball today bodes well for the future of the game. Many of those girls will develop into players who will match and even exceed the accomplishments of current players—the college and WNBA players who serve as their role models today.

The game of women's basketball has not come close to reaching its peak. The coaches and players are ever working to improve themselves and the game. Women players will get taller, stronger and quicker. They will set records and will, as some of their predecessors did, challenge men's teams and be able to hold their own.

The coaches, past and present, have achieved greatness and have provided the groundwork for a productive future for women's basketball.

# *Notes*

## Preface

1. Jody Conradt, "Foreword," in Joan S. Hult and Marianna Trekell, eds., *A Century of Women's Basketball: From Frailty to Final Four* (Reston, Va.: National Association for Girls and Women in Sport, 1991), ix.

2. Bob Herzog, "100 Years of Hoopla," *Newsday*, Nassau and Suffolk ed., Jan. 5, 1992, Sports; Sunday Special, 16 (other ed., City, 14).

3. Anderson, Kelli, "Star Power," *Sports Illustrated for Women*, Spring 1999, 56–59.

4. Frank Dell'apa, "Basketball's Centennial; In the Beginning; Dr. James Naismith's Basket Ball Discovery Solid as a Rock," *The Houston Chronicle*, Dec. 22, 1991, Sports, 12.

## Introduction

1. Bernadette V. McGlade (assistant commissioner Women's Basketball Operations, ACC), interview by the author, Aug. 26, 1999.

2. Cheryl Miller, email interview, by the author, Aug. 24, 1999.

3. Christine H. B. Grant, interview by the author, Sept. 1, 1999; Christine H. B. Grant, resume, Sept. 1, 1999.

4. William F. Reed, "Here's How It's Done, Guys: Bernadette Lock Becomes First Female Coach in Division I Basketball: Scorecard," *Sports Illustrated* (June 25, 1990), 72:26, 12(1).

5. R. Vivian Acosta and Linda Jean Carpenter, "Women in Intercollegiate Sport: A Longitudinal Study—Twenty-One Year Update 1977–1998"

(Brooklyn, N.Y.: Department of Physical Education and Exercise Science, CUNY, 1998), 1.

# Chapter 1

1. Alice W. Frymir, *Basket Ball for Women* (New York: A.S. Barnes, 1928), 30.

2. Constance Nelson and Billy Steve Clayton, "College Basketball: The First 100 Years," *Minneapolis Star Tribune*, Mar. 29, 1992, C20; Bob Herzog, "100 Years of Hoopla," *Newsday*, Nassau and Suffolk ed., Jan. 5, 1992, Sports, 16 (other ed., City, 14).

3. Ron Thomas, "Cal vs. Stanford in 1896: Women's Game Is Born," *The San Francisco Chronicle*, Jan. 10, 1992, E1; "A Brief History of Basketball," *The Christian Science Monitor*, Dec. 27, 1991, Sports, 10.

4. Frank Dell'apa, "Basketball's Centennial: In the Beginning; Dr. James Naismith's Basket Ball Discovery Solid as a Rock," *The Houston Chronicle*, Dec. 22, 1991, Sports, 12.

5. Janice A. Beran, *From Six-on-Six to Full Court Press: A Century of Iowa Girls' Basketball* (Ames: Iowa State University Press, 1993), 1st ed., 4. The WNBA website says the score of the April 1 game was 2–1.

6. Quoted by Thomas, "Cal vs. Stanford in 1896."

7. Thomas, "Cal vs. Stanford in 1896."

8. Joan S. Hult and Marianna Trekell, eds., *A Century of Women's Basketball: From Frailty to Final Four* (Reston, Va.: National Association for Girls and Women in Sport, 1991), 427.

9. "Ten Coaches You Should Know," *News and Features: National Women's History Month*, WNBA and ESPN, 1998. Available http://www.wnba.com/features/ten_coaches.html.

10. Beran, *From Six-on Six*, 6–7.

11. Sally Jenkins, "From Berenson to Bolton, Women's Hoops Has Been Rising for 100 Years," *News and Features: National Women's History Month*, WNBA, 1999. Available: http://www.wnba.com/news/jenkins_feature.html.

12. Frymir, *Basket Ball for Women*, 43–44, 224.

13. Jenkins, "From Berenson to Bolton."

14. Tom Weir, "Hoops Pioneers Get Home Court," *USA Today*, June 3, 1999, C3.

15. Weir, "Hoops Pioneers."

16. "Ten Players You Should Know: Though Not Household Names, These Women Have Made Their Mark," *News and Features: National Women's History Month*, WNBA and ESPN, 1998. Available: http://www.wnba.com/features/ten_players.html.

17. Jenkins, "From Berenson to Bolton."

18. Herzog, "100 Years of Hoopla."

# Chapter 2

1. Angie Lee, interview by the author, May 13, 1999.

2. Charles E. Mariske, Steven Vagi, and Arlene Taick, "Combatting Sexual Harassment: A New Awareness," *USA Today* [magazine] **108**, no. 2418 (March 1980): 46.

3. Rosemary Bryant Mariner, "A Soldier Is a Soldier," *Joint Force Quarterly* **3** (Winter 1993-94): 54–61.

4. 20 U.S.C. § 1681(a).

5. Mark Conrad, "Title IX and Sports: 25 Years Later," *New York Law Journal* (June 27, 1997), 5.

6. The Feminist Majority Foundation and New Media Publishing Inc., "Women in Sports and the Olympics, Increasing Girls' and Women's Sports Opportunities," 1996. Available: http://www.feminist.org/other/olympic/caption.html#title.

7. Conrad, "Title IX and Sports."

8. 34 C.F.R. § 106.41(b) (1993).

9. Policy Interpretation; Title IX and Intercollegiate Athletics 44 Fed. Reg. 71,413 and 71,415 (1979).

10. R. Vivian Acosta and Linda Jean Carpenter, "Women in Intercollegiate Sport: A Longitudinal Study—Twenty-One Year Update 1977–1998" (Brooklyn, N.Y.: Department of Physical Education and Exercise Science, CUNY, 1998), 1–15.

11. The Equal Pay Act of 1963, as amended, 29 U.S.C. § 206(d) and (d)(1) (1988); Title VII of the Civil Rights Act of 1964, 42 U.S.C. § 2000e to 2000e-17 (1988); Title IX, Part VI.

12. Cathryn Claussen, "Title IX and Employment Discrimination in Coaching Intercollegiate Athletics," *University of Miami Entertainment & Sports Law Review* (Fall 1994 / Spring 1995), 12, n. 5.

13. Lisa A. Bireline Sarver, "Athletics: Coaching Contracts Take on the Equal Pay Act: Can (and Should) Female Coaches Tie the Score?" *Creighton Law Review* **28** (June 1995): 885–899, 920.

14. *Stanley v. University of Southern California*, 13 F.3d 1313 (9th Cir. 1994).

15. Bob Egelko, "Court Rejects Marianne Stanley's Equal-Pay Suit," [San Francisco] *AP State and Regional*, June 3, 1999; *Stanley v. University of Southern California*, Nos. 95-55466, 95-56250, 96-55004, United States Court of Appeals for the Ninth Circuit, 178 F.3d 1069; 1999 U.S. App., June 2, 1999.

16. *Harker v. Utica College of Syracuse University*, 885 F. Supp. 378 (N.D.N.Y. 1995).

17. Janet Judge, David O'Brien, and Timothy O'Brien, "Pay Equity: A Legal and Practical Approach to the Compensation of College Coaches," *Seton Hall Journal of Sport Law* **6** (1996): 549.

18. Judge *et al.*, "Pay Equity," 556.

19. Gregory Szul, "Sports Law: Sex Discrimination and the Equal Pay Act in Athletic Coaching," *Journal of Art and Entertainment Laws* 5 (Winter, 1994/Spring, 1995): 161+.

20. P.L. 102–66 (1991).

21. Joint Hearings on H.R. 4803 before the House Subcommittees on Education and Labor and Post Office and Civil Service, reprinted in 1994 *Daily Lab. Rep.* (BNA) d27 (July 22, 1994).

22. Sandra J. Libeson, "Comment: Reviving the Comparable Worth Debate in the United States: A Look Toward the European Community," *Comparative Labor Law Journal* 16 (Spring 1995): 360.

23. H.R. 4803, 103rd Cong., 2d Sess. § (G)(1)(A), § 3(B)(4)(B) (1994), in Szul, "Sports Law," n. 70–73.

24. Don Sabo, "Gender Equity Report" Women's Sports Foundation, 1997. Available: http://www.wsf.mediapolis.com/WoSport/state/GENEQ97.

25. Ray Yasser and Samuel J. Schiller, "Gender Equity in Athletics," *Cardozo Arts & Entertainment Law Journal* (1997), 15.

26. Jeffrey Selingo and Jim Naughton, "New Federal Guidelines Seek to Define Pay Equity for Men's and Women's Coaches; Impact of the EEOC's Policy Is Likely to Be Greatest in Basketball," *Chronicle of Higher Education* (Nov. 14, 1997), A47; Equal Employment Opportunity Commission (EEOC), "Enforcement Guidance on Sex Discrimination in the Compensation of Sports Coaches in Educational Institutions," October 29, 1997, available: http://www.eeoc.gov/docs/coaches.txt; EEOC, "Policy Statement on EPA Coverage of Sports Coaches," *Fair Employment Practices Manual* (Aug. 8, 1988), § 405:5607.

27. Judge *et al.*, "Pay Equity," 554.

28. Vicki Michaelis, "Women Coaches Far from Achieving Equal Pay," *Denver Post*, Dec. 8, 1998, D12.

29. "EEOC Issues Guidance on Application of Anti Discrimination Laws to Coaches' Pay at Educational Institutions," (Washington, D.C.:EEOC, Oct. 31, 1997) available: http://www.eeoc.gov/docs/coaches.txt.

30. The panelists were Alexander Wolff, *Sports Illustrated* senior writer; Dr. Judith Sweet, director of Athletics at U.C. San Diego since 1975; Jennifer McKenna, co-founder and managing director of the California Women's Law Center; and Jared W. Huffman of Boyd, Huffman & Williams, a San Francisco law firm. Linda Stoick, a San Francisco attorney with her own firm, served as moderator Bar Association of San Francisco, *The Recorder* (February 2, 1993) 10:3, Special Supplement, 5.

31. WBCA, "Basketball Coaches Survey Report," Nov. 1997.

32. WSF, "Gender Equity Report," March 1997. Available: http://www.womenssportsfoundation.org/WoSport/resource_frame.html.

33. WSF, *Report: Addressing the Needs of Female Professional and Amateur Athletes*, 1999, 2–3.

34. Judge *et al.*, "Pay Equity," 555.

35. *Haffer v. Temple University*, 678 F. Supp. 517 (E.D. Pa.); Andrew Blum, "Athletics in the Court," *National Law Journal* (April 5, 1993), 1.

36. Diane Heckman, "The Explosion of Title IX Legal Activity in Intercollegiate Athletics During 1992–93: Defining the 'Equal Opportunity Standard,'" *Detroit College of Law Review* (Fall 1994), 963.

37. *Grove City College v. Bell*, 465 U.S. 555 (1984).

38. Acosta and Carpenter, "Women in Intercollegiate Sport," 1–15.

39. Civil Rights Restoration Act of 1987, 20 U.S.C. § 1687–88 (1990); Andrew Blum, "Athletics in the Court," 1.

40. 44 Fed. Reg. 71, 413, 718 (1979).

41. John Gibeaut, "Shooting for Parity on the Playing Fields: Courts Seek Formula for Gender Equality in College Athletic Programs Under Title IX," *ABA Journal* 83 (May 1997): 40.

42. *Franklin v. Gwinnett County Public Schools*, 112 S. Ct. 1028 (1992).

43. Christine H. B. Grant, interview by the author, Sept. 1, 1999.

44. NCAA, "Revenues and Expenses of Divisions I and II Intercollegiate Athletics Programs: Financial Trends and Relationships—1997" (Overland Park, Kansas: NCAA, Oct. 1998).

45. *Roberts v. Colorado State University*, 998 F.2d 824 (10th Cir. 1993), cert. Denied, 114S.Ct. 580(1993).

46. *Cohen v. Brown University*, 991 F.2d 888 (1st Cir. 1993); 101 F.3d 155 (1996); *Cohen v. Brown University* 95-2205 (1st Cir. 1996).

47. *Brown University v. Cohen*, 96-1321, 520 U.S. 1186; 117 S. Ct. 1469; 1997 U.S. LEXIS 2554; 137 L. Ed. 2d 682; 65 U.S.L.W. 3711, April 21, 1997, Decided.

48. Steve Wulf, "A Level Playing Field for Women," *Time* (May 5, 1997), 149:18.

49. Deidre G. Duncan, "Comment: Gender-Equity in Women's Athletics," *University of Cincinnati Law Review* 64 (Spring 1996): 1055.

50. Acosta and Carpenter, "Women in Intercollegiate Sport," 4.

51. Donna Lopiano, unpublished manuscript; revision of Donna A. Lopiano, "Equity in Women's Sports: A Health and Fairness Perspective," *Clinics in Sports Medicine* 13, no. 2 (April 1994): 281–296.

52. Linda Jean Carpenter interview by the author, Aug. 24, 1999.

53. *California National Organization for Women v. Board of Trustees for the California State University*, No. 949207 (Cal. Super. Ct. San Francisco County 1993), in Heckman, "The Explosion of Title IX Legal Activity." 992.

54. *California National Organization for Women v. Evans* No. 728548 (Cal. Super. Ct. County of Santa Clara 1993) in Heckman, "The Explosion of Title IX Legal Activity." 992.

55. Jim Naughton, "Judge Approves Settlement of Brown U.'s Title IX Case," *Chronicle of Higher Education* (July 3, 1998), A31.

56. Claussen, "Title IX and Employment Discrimination,"149.

57. *Tyler v. Howard University*, No. 91-CA11239 (D.C. Super. Ct. 1993).

58. Judge *et al.*, "Pay Equity," 549 n. 2; Debra E. Blum, "2 More Coaches of Women's Teams Go to Court to Press Claims of Sex Discrimination," *The Chronicle of Higher Education* (Sept. 1, 1993), 40:2, A47, 48.

59. *Pitts v. Oklahoma*, No. CIV-93-1341-A (W.D. Okla. 1994).

60. *New York Law School Journal of Human Rights*, 347.

61. Acosta and Carpenter, "Women in Intercollegiate Sport," cited in Lopiano, unpublished manuscript. 1999.

62. Paul Reidinger, "Trends in the Law, Gender Bias: Plaintiffs Lose in 8th Circuit," *ABA Journal* **74** (Sept. 1, 1988): 92.

63. Subpart E, Title IX, 34 C.F.R. 106.51-.61 (1996); Grace-Marie Mowery, "Tenth Annual Corporate Law Symposium: Intellectual Property Law for the Twenty-first Century: Comment: Creating Equal Opportunity for Female Coaches: Affirmative Action under Title IX," *University of Cincinnati Law Review* **66** (Fall 1997): 283–287, 314–315.

64. *Perdue v. City University of New York*, 13 F. Supp. 2d 326 (E.D.N.Y. 1998).

65. *Lowrey v. Texas A & M University in System*, 11 F. Supp. 2d 895 (S.D. Tex. 1998); "Recent Developments in the Law: Universities and Other Institutions of Higher Learning," *Journal of Law and Education* **28** (April 1999): 285.

66. Mike Fish, "Women in Sports: Growing Pains; Under Fire," *Atlanta Constitution* (Sept. 23, 1998), D08.

67. Jeff Schultz, "Tech, Dogs Progressing with Title IX," *Atlanta Journal and Constitution*, Mar. 12, 1992, E3.

68. Lauren Kessler, *Full Court Press: A Season in the Life of a Winning Basketball Team and the Women Who Made It Happen* (New York: Dutton, 1997), 25.

69. Landon Hall, "Runge, Oregon Agree to Four-Year Contract," AP, Portland, Ore., April 29, 1999.

70. Tonya M. Evans, "In the Title IX Race Toward Gender-Equity, the Black Female Athlete Is Left to Finish Last: The Lack of Access for the 'Invisible Woman,'" *Howard Law Journal* **42** (Fall 1998): 105, 118, 121.

71. Evans, "In the Title IX Race,"123.

72. "Women Basketball Coaches: Grooming the Overlooked Stars of the Collegiate Sports World," *Ebony* (April 1994), 49:6, 122–126.

73. C. Bonnie Everhart and Packianathan Chelladuria, "Gender Differences in Preferences for Coaching as an Occupation: The Role of Self-efficacy, Valence, and Perceived Barriers," *Research Quarterly for Exercise and Sport* **69** no. 2 (June 1998): 118ff (13 pages).

74. Acosta and Carpenter (1988), in Everhart and Chelladuria, "Gender Differences in Preferences."

75. T. W. Caccese and C. K. Mayerberg, "Gender Differences in Perceived Burnout of College Coaches," *Journal of Sport Psychology* 6 (1984): 279–288 in Everhart and Chelladuria, "Gender Differences in Preferences."

76. B. L. Parkhouse and J.M. Williams, "Differential Effects of Sex and Status on Evaluation of Coaching Ability," *Research Quarterly for Exercise and Sport* (1986), 57: 1, and Weinberg, Revels, and Jackson, "Attitudes of Male and Female Athletes Toward Male and Female Coaches," *Journal of Sport Psychology* 6 (1984): 448–553 in Everhart and Chelladuria, "Gender Differences in Preferences."

77. R. V. Acosta and L.J. Carpenter, "Status of Women in Athletics—Changes and Causes," *Journal of Physical Education, Recreation and Dance* (1985), 56(6): 35–37, and S. True, "Percentages of Girls' High School Athletic Teams Coached by Women," Kansas City, MO.: National Federation of State High School Associations (1983), in Everhart and Chelladuria, "Gender Differences in Preferences."

78. R. M Kanter, *Men and Women in the Corporation*, New York: Basic Books(1977) and D. J. Lovett and C. D. Lowry, "'Good Old Boys' and 'Good Old Girls' Clubs: Myth or Reality?" *Journal of Sport Management* 8 (1994): 27–35, and J. M Stangl and M. J. Kane, "Structural Variables That Offer Explanatory Power for the Underrepresentation of Women Coaches Since Title IX: The Case of Homologous Reproduction," *Sociology of Sport Journal* 8 (1991): 47–60, in Everhart and Chelladuria, "Gender Differences in Preferences."

79. B. Hart, C. Hasbrook, and S. Mathes, "An Examination of the Reduction in the Number of Female Interscholastic Coaches," *Research Quarterly for Exercise and Sport* 57 (1986): 68–77, in Everhart and Chelladuria, "Gender Differences in Preferences."

80. M. R. Weiss and C. Stevens, "Motivation and Attrition of Female Coaches: An Application of Social Exchange Theory," *The Sport Psychologist* 7 (1993): 244–261 (1993), in Everhart and Chelladuria, "Gender Differences in Preferences."

81. Grant, interview

82. McGlade, interview by the author, Aug. 26, 1999.

83. Ceal Barry, interview by the author, Sept. 2, 1999.

84. Rene Portland, interview by the author, Sept. 3, 1999.

85. Barbara Stevens, interview by the author, Aug. 24, 1999.

86. Grant, interview.

87. Donna A. Lopiano, interview by the author, Aug. 25, 1999.

88. Debra E. Blum, "Trailblazer: Community College has Nation's First Female Head Coach for Men's Basketball," *Chronicle of Higher Education* (Mar. 8, 1996), A36.

89. Detroit Shock, "Head Coach Nancy Lieberman-Cline," WNBA and/or ESPN, 1998. Available: http://www.wnba.com/shock/coach.html.

90. Charles S. Farrell, "Basketball Coaches Assail Scholarship Cuts," *Chronicle of Higher Education* (Feb. 18, 1987), 33, 31+.

91. Robert Sullivan, "A Law That Needs New Muscle," *Sports Illustrated* (Mar. 4, 1985), 9, in *New York Law School Journal of Human Rights*, "Note: The Opportunity to Play Ball: Title IX, University Compliance, and Equal Pay" 13, no. 4 (Winter 1997): 348.

92. Wayne Coffey, "Money's the Missing Ingredient," [*New York*] *Daily News*, July 18, 1999, Sports, 91.

93. Egelko, "Court Rejects Marianne Stanley's Equal-Pay Suit."

94. Michaelis, "Women Coaches."

95. Michaelis, "Women Coaches."

96. *Regents of the University of California v. Bakke*, No. 76-811, 438 U.S. 265; 98 S. Ct. 2733; 1978; *O'Conner v. Board of Education of School District 23*, No. A-384, 449 U.S. 1301; 101 S. Ct. 72; 1980, Ed. 2d 179; 49 *U.S.L.W.* 3351, Nov. 4, 1980, Decided 57 L. Ed. 2d 750; 17 *Fair Employment Practice Cases* (BNA) 1000; 17 *Employment Practice Decisions* (CCH) P8402, October 12, 1977, Argued, June 28, 1978, Decided.

97. Lynn Bria, interview by the author, Aug. 31, 1999.

98. USDE, OCR, "Title IX: 25 Years of Progress," July 9, 1997. Available: http://www.ed.gov/pubs/TitleIX/title.htm.

# Chapter 3

1. Donna A. Lopiano, "Women's Sports: Coming of Age in the Third Millennium," unpublished manuscript.

2. Bob Herzog, "100 Years of Hoopla," *Newsday*, Nassau and Suffolk ed., Jan. 5, 1992, Sports, 16 (other ed., City, 14); "A Brief History of Basketball," *The Christian Science Monitor*, Dec. 27, 1991, Sports, 10.

3. "The IKON/WBCA Coach of the Year Award," Women's Basketball Coaches Association, Lilburn, Georgia, 1999. Available: http://wbca.org/html/awards/html/COY.html.

4. Rob Stein, UPI (Springfield, Mass.), Oct. 23, 1984, Regional News.

5. Ken Ross, "Women Break into Basketball Hall of Fame," UPI, (Springfield, Mass.), Jul. 1, 1985, Regional News.

6. Tom Weir, "Hoops Pioneers Get Home Court," *USA Today*, June 3, 1999, C3.

7. Nancy Lieberman-Cline, "Changes to the Game," *News and Features: National Women's History Month*, WNBA and ESPN, 1998. Available: http://wnba.com/news_feat/lc_feature.html.

8. "Ten Players You Should Know: Though Not Household Names, These Women Have Made Their Mark," *News and Features: National Women's History Month*, WNBA and ESPN, 1998. Available: http://www/wnba.com/news_feat/ten_players.html.

9. "History of Women's Basketball: More Than a Century of Women's Hoops Precedes the WNBA," WNBA and ESPN, 1998. Available: http://www.wnba.com.

10. "U.S. Women's National Team Announced," *WNBA Playoffs 1999*, WNBA.com, Aug. 14, 1999. Available: http://www.wnba.com/news/usa_team2000.html.

11. Women's Basketball Coaches Association, July 6, 1999. Available: http://www.wbca.org.

12. Deidre G. Duncan, "Comment: Gender Equity in Women's Athletics," *University of Cincinnati Law Review* 64 (Spring 1996), 1043.

13. NCAA Gender-Equity Task Force, Final Report, July 26, 1993.

14. Sandy Keenan, "Women's Watchdog: Lopiano Wages Gender-Equity War with the NCAA," *Newsday*, Jan. 9, 1994, 16.

15. Walter Byers, "Unsportsmanlike Conduct: Exploiting College Athletes 3," *NCAA Manual* 1(1995-1996). in Darryl C. Wilson, "Title IX's Collegiate Sports Application Raises Serious Questions Regarding the Role of the NCAA," *The John Marshall Law Review* 31 (Summer 1998): 1303–1304.

16. "History of Women's Basketball."

17. "Q and A," *The Seattle Times*, Dec. 23, 1998, Final ed., E4; "American Basketball League Timeline," *Seattle Post-Intelligencer*, Dec. 23, 1998, Final ed., D4.

18. Daniel Kaplan, "Shelved ABL Couldn't Beat Lack of Capital, TV Coverage; American Basketball League," *Business First–Columbus* (January 1, 1999), 19:15, 9.

19. Daniel Green and Harris Collingwood, "Toss Up; Profitability of Women's Professional Sports: Women's National Basketball Association, American Basketball League," *Working Woman* (April 1997) 4:22, 26.

20. "Sports," *Mining Co. Guide to Women's History*, 1999.

21. "League's Demise Gives Rival WNBA Pick of Best from ABL Talent Pool," *The Seattle Times*, Dec. 23, 1998, E4.

22. Betty Jaynes, interview by the author, Oct. 20 and 22, 1999.

23. Gail Goestenkors, interview by the author, Aug. 24, 1999.

24. Christine H. B. Grant, interview by the author, Sept. 1, 1999.

25. Jody Conradt, interview by the author, Oct. 5, 1999.

26. Jaynes, interview.

27. Bernadette V. McGlade, interview by the author, Aug. 26, 1999.

28. Donna A. Lopiano, interview by the author, Aug. 25, 1999.

29. R. Vivian Acosta, interview by the author, Aug. 24, 1999.

30. Barbara Stevens, interview by the author, August 24, 1999.

31. "Sports," *Mining Co. Guide.*

32. Pat Summitt with Sally Jenkins, *Reach for the Summit: The Definite Dozen System for Succeeding at Whatever You Do* (New York: Broadway Books, 1998), 140, 165.

33. Pat Summitt with Sally Jenkins, *Raise the Roof: The Inspiring Inside Story of the Tennessee Lady Vols' Undefeated 1997-98 Season* (New York: Broadway Books, 1998), 17.

34. Grace-Marie Mowery, Tenth Annual Corporate Law Symposium: Intellectual Property Law for the Twenty-first Century: Comment: Creating Equal Opportunity for Female Coaches: Affirmative Action Under Title IX, *University of Cincinnati Law Review* (Fall 1997), 286.

35. Ray Yasser, quoted in David Hill, "A Price for Equity," *Teacher Magazine*, Aug. 1996, in Ray Yasser and Samuel J. Schiller, "Gender-Equity in Athletics: The New Battleground of Interscholastic Sports," *Cardozo Arts & Entertainment Law Journal* 15 (1997): 371, n.102.

36. *1993-94 Handbook of the National Federation of State High School Associations*, in Michael Straubel, "Gender-Equity, College Sports, Title IX and Group Rights: A Coach's View," *Brooklyn Law Review* 62 (Fall 1996): 1042.

37. "Participation Numbers Narrowly Miss Record," *NCAA News*, July 19, 1996, 1, 13, in Straubel, "Gender-Equity," 1042.

38. Straubel, "Gender-Equity," 1071–1074.

39. Donna A. Lopiano, unpublished manuscript; revision of "Equity in Women's Sports: A Health and Fairness Perspective," *Clinics in Sports Medicine*, 13 no. 2 (April 1994): 281–296.

40. The National Federation of State High School Associations, "1999 High School Participation Survey," 1999. Available: http://www.nfhs.org/1999_part_index.htm.

41. Nancy Hoppe, interview with author, April 19, 1999.

42. Goestenkors, interview.

43. Sharon Ginn, "Professionals, Sponsors at Final Four to Promote Sport," *St. Petersburg Times,* Mar. 23, 1997, 2C.

44. Lopiano, "Women's Sports: Coming of Age."

45 Ray Yasser and Samuel J. Schiller, "Gender Equity in Athletics: The New Battleground of Interscholastic Sports," *Cardozo Arts & Entertainment Law Journal* 15 (1997): 371.

46 Curry Kirkpatrick, "Women's Basketball: Not Just a Dream; Though Overshadowed by the Men, the U.S. Women Have a Golden Vision," *Sports Illustrated,* June 8, 1992, 40.

47. Dylan B. Tomlinson, "Edwards Is Able to Coach and Play," *The Denver Post,* Oct. 30, 1997, D08.

48. Richard M. Campbell, "Attendance Bounce... Women's Basketball Attendance Soars Past Seven Million," *The NCAA News,* Jun. 15, 1998. Available: http://www.ncaa.org/news/19980615/active/3524n01.html.

49. "Final Fours Play to the Crowds: Women's Championship Obtains Record Mark," *The NCAA News,* Apr. 12, 1999. Available: http://www.ncaa.org/news/19990412/active/3608n04.html.

50. Frank Dell'apa, "Basketball's Centennial: In the Beginning; Dr.

James Naismith's Basket Ball Discovery Solid as a Rock," *The Houston Chronicle,* Dec. 22, 1991, Sports, 12.

## Chapter 4

1. Christine H. B. Grant, interview by the author, Sept. 1, 1999.

2. Sources for this section: R. Vivian Acosta, interview by the author, Aug. 24, 1999; R. Vivian Acosta and Linda Jean Carpenter, "Women in Intercollegiate Sport: A Longitudinal Study—Twenty-One Year Update 1977–1998" (Brooklyn, N.Y.: Department of Physical Education and Exercise Science, CUNY, 1998), 1–15.

3. Sources for this section: Linda Jean Carpenter, interview by the author, Aug. 24, 1999; R. Vivian Acosta and Linda Jean Carpenter, "Women in Intercollegiate Sport: A Longitudinal Study—Twenty One Year Update 1977–1998" (Brooklyn, N.Y.: Department of Physical Education and Exercise Science, CUNY, 1998, 1–15); Ellen J. Vargas, William J. White, and Reginald Welch, "EEOC Guidance on Application of Anti-Discrimination Laws to Coaches' Pay at Educational Institutions" (Washington, D.C.: The U.S. EEOC, Oct. 31, 1997), available: http://www.eeoc.gov.

4. Sources for this section: Grant, interview; Christine H. B. Grant, resume, Sept. 1, 1999; University of Iowa Women's Athletics, "Christine H. B. Grant," 1999, available: http://www.uiowa.edu/~shlps/faculty/grant.html.

5. Sources for this section: Betty Jaynes, interview by the author, Oct. 20, 22, 1999; Betty F. Jaynes, resume, Oct. 20, 1999; WBCA, "Basketball Coaches Survey Report," Nov. 1997; WBCA, "Statistics of the WBCA Membership," May 21, 1999, available: http://www.wbca.org/html/wbca.html.

6. Sources for this section: Donna A. Lopiano, interview by the author, Aug. 25, 1999; Donna A. Lopiano, resume, Aug. 25, 1999; Don Sabo, "Gender-Equity Report," Women's Sports Foundation, 1998, available: http://www.womenssportsfoundation.org/WoSport/resource_frame.html.

7. Sources for this section: Bernadette V. McGlade, interview by the author, Aug. 26, 1999; Atlantic Coast Conference, "Bernadette V. McGlade, Associate Commissioner, Atlantic Coast Conference," fax to author, Sept. 17, 1999; staff and wire reports, "Colleges," *Durham Herald-Sun,* Oct. 2, 1997, B2.

8. Sources for this section: Sue Rodin, interview by the author, Sept. 1, 1999; Sue Rodin, resume, Aug. 26, 1999; Women in Sports and Events, "All About WISE," and "Wise Women of the Year," 1999, available: http://www.womeninsportsandevents.com, Aug. 19, 1999.

9. Sources for this section: University of Connecticut, "Women's Basketball: Meet Head Coach Geno Auriemma," Total College Sports Network, Nov. 2, 1999, available: http://www.uconnhuskies.com/bko/bkw/

bkwcoachbio.html; Ursula Reel, "Uconn, Lady Vols Give It the Old One-Two Punch," *The New York Post*, Jan. 10, 1999, Sports, 101; "College Basketball: Sales Is Given Free Shot, and Sinks It for Record," *The New York Times*, Feb. 25, 1998, C1.

10. Louisiana Tech University, "Louisiana Tech University Sports: An Interview with Lady Techster Head Coach Leon Barmore," Total College Sports Network, Nov. 11, 1999, available: http://www.latechsports.com/bko/bkw/barmoreint.html; Louisiana Tech University, "Louisiana Tech University Sports: Head Coach Leon Barmore," Total College Sports Network, Oct. 14, 1999. Available: http://www.latechsports.com/bko/bkw/bkwcoachbio.html; Ted Lewis, "Techsters' Barmore Says Season Wasn't a Total Loss," *The New Orleans Times-Picayune* , Mar. 28, 1999, C11; Vic Dorr, Jr., "Tradition of Excellence: Barmore Built Dynasty at LA Tech," *The Richmond Times Dispatch*, Dec. 6, 1997, D1.

11. Sources for this section: Tony DiCecco, interview by the author, Aug. 25, 1999; University of Northern Iowa, "2000 Panther Basketball," "Tony DiCecco—Head Women's Basketball Coach," Available: http://www.uni.edu/athletic/wbb/00dicecobio.html; Lis Erickson ,"Head Coach Tony DiCecco," *Comin' at Ya, Panthers: 1998-99 Northern Iowa Women's Basketball* (Cedar Falls: Northern Iowa Women's Basketball Athletic Media Relations Office, 1998-99), 6–7.

# Chapter 5

1. Pat Summitt with Sally Jenkins, *Reach for the Summit: The Definite Dozen System for Succeeding at Whatever You Do* (New York: Broadway Books, 1998).

2. Tony DiCecco, interview by the author, Aug. 25, 1999.

3. Pat Summitt with Sally Jenkins, *Raise the Roof: The Inspiring Inside Story of the Tennesee Lady Vols' Undefeated 1997-98 Season* (New York: Broadway Books, 1998), 223.

4. Gail Goestenkors interview by the author, Aug. 24, 1999.

5. R. Vivian Acosta and Linda Jean Carpenter, "Women in Intercollegiate Sport: A Longitudinal Study—Twenty-One Year Update 1977–1998" (Brooklyn, N.Y.: Department of Physical Education and Exercise Science, CUNY, 1998), 1–15.

6. Debra Blum, "Trailblazer: Community College Has Nation's First Female Head Coach for Men's Basketball," *The Chronicle of Higher Education* (Mar. 8, 1996) 42:26, A35–37.

7. Mark Frances Cohen, "Making It Work: The First Among Men," *New York Times,* Jan. 14, 1996, 13:3.

8. Seth Davis, "A Modest Proposal: It's Time Women Basketball Coaches Got the Chance to Run Men's College Programs," *Sports Illustrated*, June 10, 1996, R5.

9. Summitt with Jenkins, *Reach for the Summit*, 254.

10. "About the NJCAA," NCJAA Web Site. Available: http://www.njcaa.org/about.htm, July 25, 1999.

11. Kerri-Ann McTiernan, interview by author, Apr. 28, 1999.

12. McTiernan, interview.

13. Sources for this section: Ceal Barry, interview by the author, Sept. 2, 1999; Dylan B. Tomlinson, "The Most Powerful Women in Colorado Sports No. 1 Ceal Barry Put Colorado—the School and the State—on the Women's Sports Map," *Denver Post*, Dec. 23, 1997, 2nd ed., D10; Colorado Basketball, "1998-99 Colorado Basketball Celebrating Its 25th Season" and "Ceal Barry: Head Coach 16th Season," Sept. 21, 1999, available: http://buffaloes.colorado.edu/sports/wbb/barry.html; "Head Coach Ceal Barry," fax to author from Colorado Basketball, Women's Basketball, Sept. 2, 1999, 1; Dylan B. Tomlinson, "CU Extends Ceal Barry's Contract Through 2003," *Denver Post*, June 25, 1999, 2nd ed., D4.

14. Sources for this section: Lynn Bria, interview by the author, Aug. 31, 1999; Ohio University, "Lynn Bria Hired as Women's Basketball Coach," Apr. 13, 1999, available: http://www.ohiobobcats.com/news/1999/04/13/bko/bkw/935534783302.html; Ohio University, "Ohio Women's Basketball Coaches: Lynn Bria: Head Coach," 1999, available: http://www.ohiobobcats.com/bko/bkw/coaches.html.

15. Sources for this section: Jody Conradt, interview by the author, Oct. 5, 1999; "Conradt Credits Mom for Competitiveness: Texas Coach Considers Basketball Hall of Fame Election 'Humbling,'" *Abilene Daily News,* June 30, 1998; John Maher, "Hall of Fame Clears Lane for Conradt Tonight," *Austin American-Statesman*, Oct. 2, 1998, A1, A16; Chip Brown, "She Raised Her Game: Jody Conradt Had to Scrimp on Everything But Success," *Dallas Morning News,* October 3, 1998, B1, B6; "Women's Basketball." "Conradt Named to Hall of Fame," *USA Today,* June 30, 1998, available:*http://www.usatoday.com/sports/basketba/skw/skewfs32.htm,* June 30, 1999; "Texas Basketball." "Coaches and Staff." "Jody Conradt," University of Texas Media Relations FAX, Sept. 23, 1999.

16. Sources for this section: Gail Goestenkors, interview by the author, Aug. 24, 1999; Duke University Department of Athletics, "Preseason Prospectus." "Duke Head Coach: Gail Goestenkors," FAX to author, Aug. 26, 1999; David Leon Moore, "A Wistful 'Wizard' Wooden Still Longs for Basic Basketball," *USA Today*, Mar. 24, 1999, final ed., C1.

17. Sources for this section: Angie Lee, interview by the author, May 13, 1999; "Coach Angie Lee," Iowa Hawkeye Women's Basketball Report *Gazette* Online, Cedar Rapids, Iowa, 1999, available: http://www.gazetteonline.com/hawkeyes/wbasket/coach/index.htm, April 27, 1999; "Head Coach Angie Lee," University of Iowa Men's Intercollegiate Athletics, 1998. Available: http://www.hawkeyesports.com/basket/staff/lee.htm, March 27, 1999; "Christmas Eve 1977," letter from Angie Lee's

father to his children; Dan Johnson, "Lee, Iowa Iron Out Three-Year Deal: Pact Will Pay Iowa Women's Coach $140,000 This Year," *The Des Moines Register*, Oct. 30, 1998, Sports, 1.

18. Sources for this section: Nancy Lieberman-Cline, "Changes to the Game: Detroit's Head Coach Sees a Bright Future for Women's Hoops," *News and Features: National Women's History Month,* WNBA.com, 1998, available: http://www.wnba.com/news_feat/lc_feature.html; Detroit Shock, "Award Named After Lieberman-Cline: Award to Honor the Nation's Best Point Guard," WNBA and or ESPN, 1999, available: http://www.wnba.com/shock/nancy_award.html; Detroit Shock, "Head Coach Nancy Lieberman-Cline," WNBA and or ESPN, 1998, available: http://www.wnba.com/shock/coach.html; "Basketball Hall of Fame: Nancy Lieberman-Cline," the Naismith Memorial Basketball Hall of Fame, Inc., 1999, available:http://www.hoophall.com/enshrinees/bio.cfm? name=NancyLiebermanCline&hardcode=no.

19. Sources for this section: Britt Robson, "Tough Talk, Tough Love," *MPLS.ST.PAUL*, February 1999, 85–87, 215–217; "Gopher Sports News: Gophers Hire Littlejohn as Women's Basketball Coach," University of Minnesota, Minneapolis, Women's Intercollegiate Athletics, Sports Information Office, April 10, 1997; "Cheryl Littlejohn, Head Women's Basketball Coach, University of Minnesota," packet from University of Minnesota Women's Athletics, Minneapolis, Aug. 19, 1999; University of Minnesota Golden Gopher Sports, "Gopher Sport News: Gophers Close Their 1998-99 Season at the Big Ten Tournament," Mar. 1, 1999, available: http://www.gophers.../press_release.asp?news_id=1739&sport_id =wbasket&TArch=&Ac_Yr, Nov. 22, 1999; Pam Schmid, "Gophers Women Basketball Preview: New Guards Put Hope on Gopher's Horizon," *Minneapolis Star Tribune*, Nov. 17, 1998, C1; Pam Schmid, "College Basketball Preview 1999-2000: One for All: 'U Looks to Ace Chemistry and Basketball,'" *Minneapolis Star Tribune*, Nov. 17, 1999, C1.

20. Sources for this section: Cheryl Miller, e-mail interview by the author, Aug. 24, 1999; Infoplease.com, "Sports – Halls of Fame/Who's Who – K-M: Cheryl Miller," Lycos, Inc., 1999, available: http://lycos.info-please.com/ipsa/A0109455.html; the Official Site of the Phoenix Mercury, "Cheryl Miller: Head Coach/General Manager, Phoenix Mercury," WNBA, 1998, available: http://www.wnba.com/mercury/coach.html, Aug. 19, 1999; "10 Players You Should Know," *News and Features: National Women's History Month* WNBA and ESPN, 1998, available: http://www.wnba.com/mercury/coach.html; Nov. 7, 1999; "Mercury Coach Signs Extension," *The Tampa Tribune*, Florida ed., Jul. 28, 1999, S3; "Cheryl Miller," *Turner Sports,* Oct. 1999, available: http://nba.com.ontheair/00421325.html.

21. Sources for this section: "Basketball Hall of Fame: Billie Moore," the Naismith Memorial Basketball Hall of Fame, Inc., 1999, available:

http://www.hoophall.com/enshrinees/bio.cfm?name=BillieMoore&hard-code=no; Trudy Tynan, "Billie Moore Recalls the Earlier Days of the Women's Game," *AP*, Springfield, Mass., Oct. 1, 1999, Sports News; Earl Gustkey, "Coaching Is No Longer a Slice of Life for This Hall of Famer; Basketball: Moore, Who Won National Women's Titles at Fullerton and UCLA, Has Made Golf a Priority Since 1993 Retirement," *Los Angeles Times*, Oct. 1, 1999, D16.

22. Sources for this section: Rene Portland, interview by the author, Sept. 3, 1999; Lady Lions Penn State Basketball, "Meet Coach Portland," September 16, 1999, available: http://www.psu.edu/sports/basketball/women/portalnd.html, Sept. 19, 1999; "WBCA Coaches to Meet with Congress at Title IX Hearings May 9," *Business Wire*, Atlanta, May 3, 1995. Portland represented WBCA—but perhaps was not sworn in. She was there.

23. University of California Women's Basketball, "Marianne Stanley: Profile," 1999, available: http://www.fansonly.com/schools/cal/sports/w-baskbl/mtt/stanley_marianne00.html, Nov. 25, 1999; "Sports People: Basketball: Stanley Fired at Cal," *The New York Times*, Late ed., Apr. 12, 1996, B15; "WBCA Addresses Stanley Equity Case," *Business Wire*, Atlanta, Sept. 16, 1993; Jane Gottesman, "Perspectives: An Odyssey of Championships and Hardships," *The New York Times*, Late ed., Nov. 19, 1995, 8–11; Nancy Gay, "Starting Over at Cal Women's Basketball: Stanley Closer to Equity After Firing, Freeze-out," *The San Francisco Chronicle*, Final ed., Nov. 13, 1996, D1; Bob Egelko, "Court Rejects Marianne Stanley's Equal Pay Suit," *AP State and Local Wire*, San Francisco, Jun. 3, 1999; Bill Shaikin, "Stanley Coach Again and Standing Her (New) Ground," Nando.net, 1996, available: http://www.news-observer.com/newsroom/sports/bkb/1996/col/bkw/feat/arc.../bkw10938.htm, Nov. 25, 1999; *Stanley V. University of Southern California*, Nos. 95-55466, 95-56250, 96-55004, United States Court of Appeals for the Ninth Circuit, 178 F.3d 1069; 1999 U.S. App. LEXIS 11170; 79 Fair Empl. Prac. Cas. (BNA) 1616; 138 Lab. Cas. (CCH) P33,881; 99 Cal. Daily Op. Service 4192, October 7, 1996, Argued and Submitted, Pasadena, California; November 28, 1997, Submission withdrawn; May 24, 1999, Resubmitted, June 2, 1999, Filed.

24. Sources for this section: Barbara Stevens, interview by the author, Aug. 24, 1999; Bentley Sports Information, "Barbara Stevens, Women's Basketball Coach, Bentley College," Aug. 13, 1999, 1.

25. Sources for this section: "Rutgers Basketball: Head Coach C. Vivian Stringer," and "Stringer's Awards and Honors: Maria Rodriguez, Sports Media Rutgers, fax, June 2, 1999; "The Stringer File," Scarlet Knights Women's Basketball Coaches, Feb 15, 1999, available: http://wysi-wyg://bball_main.18http://ath...ketball-women/coaches/stringer.htm, May 21, 1999; Linda Robertson, "Circle of Life," *Sports Illustrated*, Spring 1997, Woman Sport, 94; Claire Smith, "College Basketball: A Coaching

Legend Comes Home; Personal Loss Spurs Stringer's Move to Help Rutgers Rebuild," *The New York Times,* Dec. 10, 1995, S. 8, 1; "Vivian Stringer Leaves Iowa to Coach Women's Basketball at Rutgers," *Jet,* Aug. 7, 1995, Sports, 48; Vincent M. Mallozzi, "College Basketball; Rutgers Pays Top Dollar for New Coach," *The New York Times,* July 15, 1995, S. 1, 31.

26. Sources for this section: "NCAA Women's Tournament Champions: Women's College Basketball," Excite Sports, 1995–1999, available: http://sports.excite.com/ncaaw/info/ncaawwin; "The Summitt Quick File: Pat Summitt, University of Tennessee, 25 Years National Champions," *The Knoxville News-Sentinel,* 1996, available: http://www.goladyvols.com/womens/basketball/coaches/Summitt/index.html; "The Drive to Be the Best Started on the Farm: Women's Basketball Coach Pat Summitt," *Successful Farming* (January, 1999), 1:97, 67; "Summitt Stands Alone at Summit of Women's Game," Associated Press, Charlotte, N.C., April 1, 1996; Pat Summitt with Sally Jenkins, *Reach for the Summit: The Definite Dozen System for Succeeding at Whatever You Do* (New York: Broadway Books, 1998), 2, 4–9, 237, 251–252, 255–256, 257–260.

27. Sources for this section: Kelli Anderson, "Cardinal Rules: A Coach with an Unflinching Work Ethic, and Players Who Love It, Have Given Stanford a Winning Style," *Sports Illustrated* (Fall 1996), 158; Nancy Gay and Tara VanDerveer, "Guest Analysis: These 4 Teams Bring Offense to the Big Show," *The San Francisco Chronicle,* Final ed., Mar. 26, 1999, F2; Tara VanDerveer with Joan Ryan, *Shooting from the Outside: How a Coach and Her Olympic Team Transformed Women's Basketball* (New York: Avon Books, 1997), 6, 11, 28–29, 31–32, 38, 40, 69, 273; Stanford University Women's Basketball, "Cardinal Women's Basketball: Bio: Tara VanDerveer, Head Coach," 1999, available: http://www.fansonly.com/schools/stan/sports/w-baskbl/mtt/stan-w-baskbl-vanderveer.html.

28. "Basketball Hall of Fame: Margaret Wade," the Naismith Memorial Basketball Hall of Fame, Inc., 1999, available: http://www.hoophall.com/enshrinees/bio. cfm?name=MargaretWade&hardcode=no, Nov. 25, 1999; Trudy Tynan, *AP,* Springfield, Mass., Apr. 7, 1985, Sports News; "Sports People: Women Honored," Apr. 7, 1985, 5–7.

29. Sources for this section: Mechelle Voepel, "Winning by the Hundreds: 500 for Washington, 300 for Williams: Milestone Moments Pressure Off for KU Women," *The Kansas City Star,* Feb. 21, 1999, C1; Mechelle Voepel, "Lessons Leave Larger Legacy: KU Women's Basketball Coach Marian Washington, Who Had Led the Jayhawks' Program Since 1973, Is Seeking Her 500th Career Victory Tonight Against Iowa State," Feb. 16, 1999, C1; University of Kansas Athletics, "Head Coach Marian Washington," 1998, available: http://www.jayhawks.org/wbb/coaches–wbb/wbbwashington.html.

30. Sources for this section: North Carolina State University "Women's Basketball: Kay Yow's 25th Anniversary Celebration and Timeline," Total

Sports Network, 1999, available: http://www.gopack.com/bko/bkw/
year25.html, North Carolina State University, "Women's Basketball:
"Coach Kay Yow Chat Answers," Total Sports Network, 1999, available:
http://www.gopack.com/news/1999/11/07/bko/bkw/942019953236.html,
Nov. 27, 1999; Lee Montgomery, "Matriarch Kay Yow," *Durham Herald-Sun*, Nov. 15, 1999, D1; Tim Peeler, "Big Winner Yow Laments a Big
Void in Her Past," *Greensboro News and Record*, Jan. 7, 1999, C1.

# Bibliography

Acosta, R. Vivian. Interview by the author, Aug. 24, 1999.

_____, and Linda Jean Carpenter. "Women in Intercollegiate Sport: A Longitudinal Study—Twenty-One Year Update 1977–1998." Brooklyn, N.Y.: Department of Physical Education and Exercise Science, CUNY, 1998. 1–15.

Anderson, Kelli. "Cardinal Rules: A Coach with an Unflinching Work Ethic, and Players Who Love It, Have Given Stanford a Winning Style." *Sports Illustrated* (Fall 1996), 158.

Atlantic Coast Conference. "Bernadette V. McGlade, Associate Commissioner, Atlantic Coast Conference." FAX to author, Sept. 17, 1999.

Barnes, Mildred J. *Women's Basketball.* Boston: Allyn and Bacon, 1972.

Barry, Ceal. Interview by the author, Sept. 2, 1999.

"Basketball Hall of Fame: Billie Moore." The Naismith Memorial Basketball Hall of Fame, Inc., 1999. Available: http://www.hoophall.com/enshrinees/bio.cfm?name=BillieMoore& hardcode=no.

"Basketball Hall of Fame: Margaret Wade." The Naismith Memorial Basketball Hall of Fame, Inc., 1999. Available: http://www.hoophall.com/enshrinees/bio.cfm?name=MargaretWade&hardcode=no.

"Basketball Hall of Fame: Nancy Lieberman-Cline." The Naismith Memorial Basketball Hall of Fame, Inc., 1999. Available: http://www.hoophall.com/enshrinees/bio.cfm?name=NancyLiebermanCline&hardcode=no.

Bentley Sports Information. "Barbara Stevens, Women's Basketball Coach, Bentley College," Aug. 13, 1999.

Beran, Janice A. *From Six-on-Six to Full Court Press: A Century of Iowa Girls' Basketball*. Ames: Iowa State University Press, 1993.

Blum, Andrew. "Athletics in the Court." *The National Law Journal* (April 5, 1993), 1.

Blum, Debra E. "Trailblazer: Community College Has Nation's First Female Head Coach for Men's Basketball." *The Chronicle of Higher Education* (Mar. 8, 1996), 42:26, A35–37.

_____. "2 More Coaches of Women's Teams Go to Court to Press Claims of Sex Discrimination." *The Chronicle of Higher Education* (Sept. 1, 1993), 40:2, A47, 48.

Bria, Lynn. Interview by the author, Aug. 31, 1999.

*Brown University, et al. v. Amy Cohen*, 96-1321, 520 U.S. 1186; 117 S. Ct. 1469; 1997 U.S. LEXIS 2554; 137 L. Ed. 2d 682; 65 *U.S.L.W.* 3711, April 21, 1997, Decided.

*California National Organization for Women v. Evans* No. 728548 (Cal. Super. Ct. County of Santa Clara 1993).

Campbell, Richard M. "Attendance Bounce...Women's Basketball Attendance Soars Past Seven Million." *The NCAA News*, Jun. 15, 1998. Available: http://www.ncaa.org/news/19980615/active/3524n01.html.

Carpenter, Linda Jean. Interview by the author, Aug. 24, 1999.

"Christmas Eve 1977." Letter provided by Angie Lee.

Claussen, Cathryn. "Title IX and Employment Discrimination in Coaching Intercollegiate Athletics." *University of Miami Entertainment & Sports Law Review* (Fall 1994/Spring 1995), 12, n. 5.

*Cohen v. Brown University*, 991 F.2d 888 (1st Cir. 1993); 101 F.3d 155 (1996); *Cohen v. Brown University* 95-2205 (1st Cir. 1996). *Cohen v. Brown University*, 991 F.2d 888 (1st Cir. 1993). *Cohen v. Brown University*, 95-2205 (1st Cir. 1996). *Cohen v. Brown University*, 809 F. Supp. 978 (D. R.I.), aff'd in part, 101 F.3d 155 (1st Cir. 1996), cert. denied, 117 S. Ct. 1469 (1997).

Colorado Basketball. "Ceal Barry: Head Coach 16th Season," Sept. 21, 1999. Available: http://buffaloes.colorado.edu/sports/wbb/barry.html.

Colorado Basketball, Women's Basketball. "Head Coach Ceal Barry." FAX to author, Sept. 2, 1999, 1.

Conrad, Mark. "Title IX and Sports: 25 Years Later." *New York Law Journal* (June 27, 1997), 5.

Conradt, Jody. Interview by the author, Oct. 5, 1999.

Davis, Seth. "A Modest Proposal: It's Time Women Basketball Coaches Got the Chance to Run Men's College Programs." *Sports Illustrated* (June 10, 1996), R5.

DeJulio, Maria. Interview by the author, May 27, 1999.

Detroit Shock. "Head Coach Nancy Lieberman-Cline." WNBA and or ESPN, 1998. Available: http://www.wnba.com/shock/coach.html.

DiCecco, Tony. Interview by the author, Aug. 25, 1999.

"The Drive to Be the Best Started on the Farm: Women's Basketball Coach Pat Summitt." *Successful Farming* (January 1999), 1:97, 67.

Duke University Department of Athletics. "Preseason Prospectus: Duke Head Coach Gail Goestenkors." FAX to author, Aug. 26, 1999.

Duncan, Deidre G. "Comment: Gender Equity in Women's Athletics." *University of Cincinnati Law Review 64* (Spring 1996): 1027–1055.

Equal Employment Opportunity Commission (EEOC). "Enforcement Guidance on Sex Discrimination in the Compensation of Sports Coaches in Educational Institutions," October 29, 1997. Available: http://www.eeoc.gov/docs/coaches.txt.

_____. "Policy Statement on EPA Coverage of Sports Coaches." *Fair Employment Practices Manual* (Aug. 8, 1988), § 405:5607.

Erickson, Lis. "Head Coach Tony DiCecco." *Comin' at Ya, Panthers: 1998–99 Northern Iowa Women's Basketball*. Cedar Falls: Northern Iowa Women's Basketball Athletic Media Relations Office, 1998–1999. 6–7.

Evans, Tonya M. "In the Title IX Race Toward Gender Equity, the Black Female Athlete Is Left to Finish Last: The Lack of Access for the 'Invisible Woman.'" *Howard Law Journal 42* (Fall 1998): 105–128.

Everhart, C. Bonnie, and Packianathan Chelladuria. "Gender Differences in Preferences for Coaching as an Occupation: The Role of Self-Efficacy, Valence, and Perceived Barriers." *Research Quarterly for Exercise and Sport 69*, no. 2 (June 1998): 188+ (13 pages).

Farrell, Charles S. "Basketball Coaches Assail Scholarship Cuts." *Chronicle of Higher Education 33* (Feb. 18, 1987): 31+.

"Final Fours Play to the Crowds: Women's Championship Obtains Record Mark." *The NCAA News*, Apr. 12, 1999. Available: http://www.ncaa.org/news/19990412/active/3608n04.html.

Fish, Mike. "Women in Sports: Growing Pains; Under Fire." *Atlanta Constitution* (Sept. 23, 1998), D08.

*Franklin v. Gwinnett County Public Schools*, 112 S. Ct. 1028 (1992).

Frymir, Alice W. *Basket Ball for Women*. New York: A.S. Barnes and Company, 1928.

Gibeaut, John. "Shooting for Parity on the Playing Fields: Courts Seek Formula for Gender Equality in College Athletic Programs Under Title IX." *ABA Journal 83* (May 1997): 40.

Goestenkors, Gail. Interview by the author, Aug. 24, 1999.

Grant, Christine H. B. Interview by the author, Sept. 1, 1999.

Green, Daniel, and Harris Collingwood. "Toss Up: Profitability of Women's Professional Sports; Women's National Basketball Association, American Basketball League." *Working Woman 4* (April 1997) 22, 26.

*Grove City College v. Bell*, 465 U.S. 555 (1984).

*Haffer v. Temple University*, 678 F. Supp. 517 (E.D. Pa.).

*Harker v. Utica College of Syracuse University*, 885 F. Supp. 378 (N.D.N.Y. 1995).

Heckman, Diane. "The Explosion of Title IX Legal Activity in Intercollegiate Athletics During 1992–93: Defining the 'Equal Opportunity Standard.'" *Detroit College of Law Review 953* (Fall 1994): 963.

Hoppe, Nancy. Interview by the author, April 19, 1999.

Hult, Joan S., and Marianna Trekell, eds. *A Century of Women's Basketball: From Frailty to Final Four*. Reston, Va.: National Association for Girls and Women in Sport, 1991.

Hunley, Tom C. In "Leader of the Pack," *The Village Voice*, Aug. 26, 1997, Letters, 6.

Jaynes, Betty. Interview by the author, Oct. 20, 22, 1999.

Jenkins, Sally. "From Berenson to Bolton, Women's Hoops Has Been Rising for 100 Years." *National Women's History Month*, WNBA, 1999. Available: http://www.wnba.com/news/jenkins_feature.html.

Judge, Janet, David O'Brien, and Timothy O'Brien. "Pay Equity: a Legal and Practical Approach to the Compensation of College Coaches." *Seton Hall Journal of Sport Law* 6 (1996): 549–580.

Kaplan, Daniel. "Shelved ABL Couldn't Beat Lack of Capital, TV Coverage; American Basketball League." *Business First–Columbus* (January 1, 1999), 19:15, 9.

Kessler, Lauren. *Full Court Press: A Season in the Life of a Winning Basketball Team and the Women Who Made It Happen*. New York: Dutton, 1997.

Lee, Angie. Interview by the author, May 13, 1999.

Libeson, Sandra J. "Comment: Reviving the Comparable Worth Debate in the United States: A Look Toward the European Community." *Comparative Labor Law Journal* 16 (Spring 1995): 358–398.

Lieberman-Cline, Nancy. "Changes to the Game." *News and Features: National Women's History Month*." WNBA and ESPN, 1998. Available: http://wnba.com/news_feat/lc_feature.html.

Lopiano, Donna A. Unpublished manuscript. Revision of Donna A. Lopiano, "Equity in Women's Sports: A Health and Fairness Perspective." *Clinics in Sports Medicine 13*, no. 4 (April 1994): 281–296.

_____. Interview by the author, Aug. 25, 1999.

_____. Resume, Aug. 25, 1999.

_____. "Women's Sports: Coming of Age in the Third Millennium." Unpublished manuscript.

"Louisiana Tech University Sports: Head Coach Leon Barmore." Total College Sports Network, Oct. 14, 1999. Available: http://www.latechsports.com/bko/bkw/bkwcoachbio.html.

"Louisiana Tech University Sports: An Interview with Lady Techster Head Coach Leon Barmore." Total College Sports Network, Nov. 11, 1999. Available: http://www.latechsports.com/bko/bkw/barmoreint.html.

*Lowrey v. Texas A & M University in System*, 11 F. Supp. 2d 895 (S.D. Tex. 1998).

McGlade, Bernadette V. Interview by the author, Aug. 26, 1999.

McTiernan, Kerri-Ann. Interview by the author, Apr. 28, 1999.

Mariner, Rosemary Bryant. "A Soldier Is a Soldier." *Joint Force Quarterly 3* (Winter 1993–94): 54–61.

Mariske, Charles E., Steven Vagi, and Arlene Taick. "Combating Sexual Harassment: A New Awareness." *USA Today* [magazine], March 1980, 45–48.

Miller, Cheryl. E-mail interview by the author, Aug. 24, 1999.

Mowery, Grace-Marie. "Comment: Creating Equal Opportunity for Female Coaches: Affirmative Action Under Title IX." *University of Cincinnati Law Review 66* (Fall 1997): 283–315.

National Association of Collegiate Directors of Athletics. *The 1998–99 National Directory of College Athletics. (Women's Edition)*. Cleveland, Ohio: Collegiate Directories, Inc., 1998.

National Collegiate Athletic Association. "Gender-Equity Study: Summary of Results," April 1997, 1–104.

_____. "Gender-Equity Task Force, Final Report," July 26, 1993.

_____. *"1997–98 NCAA Gender-Equity Study,"* Oct. 1999.

_____. "Revenues and Expenses of Divisions I and II Intercollegiate Athletics Programs: Financial Trends and Relationships—1997." Overland Park, Kansas: NCAA, Oct. 1998.

National Federation of State High School Associations. "1999 High School Participation Survey." Available: http://www.nfhs.org/1999_part_index.html.

Naughton, Jim. "Judge Approves Settlement of Brown U.'s Title IX Case." *Chronicle of Higher Education* (July 3, 1998), A31.

North Carolina State University. "Women's Basketball: Coach Kay Yow Chat Answers." Total Sports Network, 1999. Available: http://www.gopack.com/news/1999/11/07/bko/bkw/942019953236.html.

_____. "Women's Basketball: Kay Yow's 25th Anniversary Celebration and Timeline." Total Sports Network, 1999. Available: http://www.gopack.com/bko/bkw/year25.html.

"Note: The Opportunity to Play Ball: Title IX, University Compliance, and Equal Pay." *New York Law School Journal of Human Rights 13* (Winter 1997): 347–410.

*O'Conner v. Board of Education of School District 23*, No. A-384, 449 U.S. 1301; 101 S. Ct. 72; 1980, Ed. 2d 179.

Ohio University. "Ohio Women's Basketball Coaches: Lynn Bria: Head Coach." 1999. Available: http://www.ohiobobcats.com/bko/bkw/coaches.html.

Pennsylvania State University. "Meet Coach Portland," September 16, 1999. Available: http://www.psu.edu/sports/basketball/women/portland.html.

*Perdue v. City University of New York*, 13 F. Supp. 2d 326 (E.D.N.Y. 1998).

Phoenix Mercury. "Cheryl Miller: Head Coach/General Manager, Phoenix Mercury." WNBA, 1998. Available: http://www.wnba.com/mercury/coach.html.

*Pitts v. Oklahoma*, No. CIV-93-1341-A (W.D. Okla. 1994).

Portland, Rene. Interview by the author, Sept. 3, 1999.

"Recent Developments in the Law: Universities and Other Institutions of Higher Learning." *Journal of Law and Education* 28 (April 1999): 282–288.

Reed, William F. "Here's How It's Done, Guys: Bernadette Lock Becomes First Female Coach in Division I Basketball." *Sports Illustrated 72*, no. 26 (June 25, 1990), 72:26, 12.

Reidinger, Paul. "Gender Bias: Plaintiffs Lose in 8th Circuit." *ABA Journal 74* (Sept. 1, 1988): 92.

*Roberts v. Colorado State University*, 998 F.2d 824 (10th Cir. 1993), cert. Denied, 114S.Ct. 580(1993).

Robertson, Linda. "Circle of Life." *Sports Illustrated* (Spring 1997), 94.

Robson, Britt. "Tough Talk, Tough Love." *MPLS.ST.PAUL*, February 1999, 85–87, 215–217.

Rodin, Sue. Interview by the author, Sept. 1, 1999.

Rodriguez, Maria. "Rutgers Basketball: Head Coach C. Vivian Stringer," and "Stringer's Awards and Honors." Sports Media-Rutgers, FAX, June 2, 1999.

Sabo, Don. "Gender Equity Report." Women's Sports Foundation, 1998. Available: http://www.womenssportsfoundation.org/WoSport/resource_frame.html.

Sarver, Lisa A. Bireline. "Athletics: Coaching Contracts Take on the Equal Pay Act: Can (and Should) Female Coaches Tie the Score?" *Creighton Law Review* 28 (June 1995): 885–899, 920.

Schultz, Jeff. "Tech, Dogs Progressing with Title IX," *Atlanta Journal and Constitution* (Mar. 12, 1992), E3.

Selingo, Jeffrey, and Jim Naughton. "New Federal Guidelines Seek to Define Pay Equity for Men's and Women's Coaches: Impact of the EEOC's Policy Is Likely to Be Greatest in Basketball." *Chronicle of Higher Education* (November 14, 1997), A47.

Simmons, Sue, and Matt Lauer. "Live at Five." WNBC Television, New York, Feb. 6, 1996.

Stanford University Women's Basketball. "Cardinal Women's Basketball: Bio: Tara VanDerveer, Head Coach." 1999. Available: http://www.fansonly.com/schools/stan/sports/w-baskbl/mtt/stan-w-baskbl-vanderveer.html.

*Stanley v. University of Southern California*, 13 F.3d 1313 (9th Cir. 1994); 79 Fair Empl. Prac. Cas. (BNA) 1616; 138 Lab. Cas. (CCH) P33,881; 99 Cal. Daily Op. Service 4192, October 7, 1996.

*Stanley v. University of Southern California*, Nos. 95-55466, 95- 56250, 96-55004, United States Court of Appeals for the Ninth Circuit, 178 F.3d 1069; 1999 U.S. App., June 2, 1999.

Stevens, Barbara. Interview by the author, Aug. 24, 1999.

Straubel, Michael. "Gender Equity, College Sports, Title IX and Group Rights: A Coach's View." *Brooklyn Law Review* 62 (Fall 1996): 1039–1074.

"The Stringer File." Scarlet Knights Women's Basketball Coaches. Feb. 15, 1999. Available: http://wysiwyg://bball_main.18http://ath...ketball-women/coaches/stringer.htm. May 21, 1999.

Suggs, Welch. "Colleges Consider Fairness of Cutting Men's Teams to Comply with Title IX." *The Chronicle of Higher Education* (Feb. 19, 1999), A53.

Summitt, Pat, with Sally Jenkins. *Raise the Roof: The Inspiring Inside Story of the Tennessee Lady Vols.' Undefeated 1997–98 Season.* New York: Broadway Books, 1998.

_____, with _____. *Reach for the Summit: The Definite Dozen System for Succeeding at Whatever You Do.* New York: Broadway Books, 1998.

Szul, Gregory. "Sports Law: Sex Discrimination and the Equal Pay Act in Athletic Coaching." *Journal of Art and Entertainment Law 5* (Winter 1994/Spring 1995): 161+.

*Tyler v. Howard University*, No. 91-CA11239 (D.C. Super. Ct. 1993).

U.S. Code, Title 20, § 1681(a).

_____, Title 20 § 1681 (1995), Part VI, Title IX, the 1972 Educational Amendments to the Civil Rights Act of 1964. Pub L. No. 92-318.

_____, Title 20, § 1687-88 (1990), Title Civil Rights Restoration Act of 1987.

_____, Title 29, § 206(d) (1995), Equal Pay Act of 1963, as amended to the Fair Labor Standards Act.

_____, Title 42, § 2000e to 2000e-17 (1988), et seq. (1995), Title VII of the Civil Rights Act of 1964.

_____, P.L. 102-166 (1991) Civil Rights Act of 1991.

U. S. Congress. House. Committee on Economic and Educational Opportunities. *Hearing on Title IX of the Education Amendments of 1972,* 104th Cong., 1st sess., May 9, 1995.

U.S. Department of Education. Office for Civil Rights. "Title IX: 25 Years of Progress," July 9, 1997. Available: http://www.ed.gov/pubs/TitleIX/title.html.

*University of California v. Bakke*, No. 76-811, 438 U.S. 265; 98 S. Ct. 2733; 1978; 57 L. Ed. 2d 750; 17 Fair Empl. Prac. Cas. (BNA) 1000; 17 Empl. Prac. Dec. (CCH) P8402, Oct. 12, 1977, Argued, June 28, 1978, Decided.

University of California Women's Basketball. "Marianne Stanley: Profile." 1999. Available: http://www.fansonly.com/schools/cal/sports/w-baskbl/mtt/stanley_marianne00.html.

University of Connecticut. "Women's Basketball: Meet Head Coach Geno Auriemma." The Total College Sports Network, Nov. 2, 1999. Available: http://www.unconnhuskies.com/bko/bkw/bkwcoachbio.html.

University of Iowa Men's Intercollegiate Athletics. "Head Coach Angie Lee." 1998. Available: http://www.hawkeyesports.com/basket/staff/lee.htm.

University of Iowa Women's Athletics. "Christine H. B. Grant." 1999. Available: http://www.uiowa.edu/~shlps/faculty/grant.html.

University of Kansas Athletics. "Head Coach Marian Washington." 1998. Available: http://www.jayhawks.org/wbb/coaches_wbb/wbbwashington.html.

University of Minnesota Golden Gopher Sports. "Gophers Close Their 1998–99 Season at the Big Ten Tournament." Gopher Sport News, Mar. 1, 1999. Available: http://www.gophers.../press_release.asp?news_id=1739&sport_id=wbasket&TArch=&Ac_Yr.

University of Northern Iowa. "2000 Panther Basketball: Tony DiCecco—Head Women's Basketball Coach," 1998–1999. Available: http://www.uni.edu/athletic/wbb/00diceccobio.html.

VanDerveer, Tara, with Joan Ryan. Shooting from the Outside: How a Coach and Her Olympic Team Transformed Women's Basketball. New York: Avon Books, 1997.

Vargas, Ellen J., William J. White, and Reginald Welch. "EEOC Guidance on Application of Anti-Discrimination Laws to Coaches' Pay at Educational Institutions." Washington, D.C.: U.S. EEOC, Oct. 31, 1997. Available: http://www.eeoc.gov.

"Vivian Stringer Leaves Iowa to Coach Women's Basketball at Rutgers." Jet, Aug. 7, 1995, 48.

Wilson, Darryl C. "Title IX's Collegiate Sports Application Raises Serious Questions Regarding The Role of The NCAA." John Marshall Law Review 31 (Summer 1998): 1303–1319.

WNBA and ESPN. "10 Players You Should Know." News and Features: National Women's History Month, WNBA and ESPN, 1998. Available: http://www.wnba.com/mercury/coach.html.

"Women Basketball Coaches: Grooming the Overlooked Stars of the Collegiate Sports World." Ebony (April 1994), 49:6, 122–126.

Women in Sports and Events. "All About WISE" and "Wise Women of the Year," 1999. Available: http://www.womeninsportsandevents.com

Women's Basketball Coaches Association. Coaching Women's Basketball. Champaign, Ill.: Human Kinetics Publishers, 1987.

_____. "Basketball Coaches Survey Report," Nov. 1997.

_____. "Statistics of the WBCA Membership," May 21, 1999. Available: http://www.wbca.org/html/wbca.html.

Women's Sports Foundation. "Gender Equity Report," March 1997. Available: http://www.womenssportsfoundation.org/WoSport/resource_frame.html.

_____. "Participation Statistics Packet," May 1999.

_____. *Report: Addressing the Needs of Female Professional and Amateur Athletes*, 1999, 1–13.

Yasser, Ray, and Samuel J. Schiller. "Gender Equity in Athletics: The New Battleground of Interscholastic Sports." *Cardozo Arts & Entertainment Law Journal 15* (1997): 371.

# Index